"The Kids Got Smarter"
Case Studies of Successful Comer Schools

UNDERSTANDING EDUCATION AND POLICY
William T. Pink and George W. Noblit
Series editors

Making Meaning of Community in an American High School
  Kathleen Knight Abowitz

Discourse and Power in Educational Organizations
  David Corson (ed.)

Flirting on the Margins (An Educational Novel)
  Robert B. Everhart

The Social Construction of Urban Schooling: Situating the Crisis
  Louis F. Mirón

Continuity and Contradiction: The Futures of the Sociology of
Education
  William T. Pink and George W. Noblit (eds.)

Caring as Tenacity: Case Studies of Urban School Survival
  Mary Anne Pitman and Debbie Zorn

Good Schools: The Policy Environment Perspective
  Charles A. Tesconi

Talking About a Revolution: The Politics and Practice of Feminist
Teaching
  Cheryl L. Sattler

Assessment and Control at Parkview School: A Qualitative Case
  Study of Accommodating Assessment Change in a Secondary School
  Hilary A. Radnor

Working Together?: Grounded Perspectives on Interagency
Collaboration
  *Amee Adkins, Catherine Awsumb, George W. Noblit, and
    Penny Richards*

A General Theory for a Democratic School
  Art Pearl and Tony Knight

Values-Spoken and Values-Lived: Race and the Cultural Consequences of a
School Closing
  Maike Philipsen

From Nihilism to Possibility:
  Democratic Transformations for Inner City Education
  Fred Yeo and Barry Kanpol (eds.)

forthcoming

From Disabling to Enabling Schools
  Roger Slee, Mel Ainscow, and Michael Hardman

"The Kids Got Smarter"
Case Studies of Successful Comer Schools

edited by

George W. Noblit
William W. Malloy
Carol E. Malloy
University of North Carolina at Chapel Hill

HAMPTON PRESS, INC.
CRESSKILL, NEW JERSEY

Printed in the United States of America

Library of Congress Cataloging-in-Publication Data

"The kids got smarter": case studies of successful Comer schools / edited by George W. Noblit, William W. Malloy, Carol E. Malloy.
    p. cm. -- (Understanding education and policy)
  Includes bibliographical references and indexes.
  ISBN 1-57273-366-7 -- ISBN 1-57273-367-5 (pbk.)
  1. School improvement programs--United States--Case studies. 2. Public schools--United States--Case studies. 3. Educational change--United States--Case studies. 4. Comer, James P. I. Title: Case studies of successful Comer Schools. II. Noblit, George W. III. Malloy, William W. IV. Malloy, Carol E. V. Series.

LB2822.82 .K52 2001
371.01--dc21

00-053575

Hampton Press, Inc.
23 Broadway
Cresskill, NJ 07626

Contents

Foreword

James P. Comer, M.D., M.P.H.

"The Kids Got Smarter" and I'm delighted—for the kids, their families, and their schools; for the realization of my dream; and because of the implications for school change.

In 1960 I returned to my hometown to do my internship, planning to become a general practitioner of medicine. But three friends who went to kindergarten with me were on a downhill life course. The question that seized me and wouldn't let go was, "Why?" They were low-income kids, but so was I. Their parents had the same kind of jobs as my parents—domestic worker and steel mill laborer. We went to the same school. And they were just as bright as anybody in my predominantly White working and upper middle-class school; and as bright as anybody in my family. My four siblings and I earned 13 college degrees.

I decided to go to the U.S. Public Health Service to do my military service and to give myself time to think. I did volunteer work at a "bootstrap" service organization helping people who had been thrown off the welfare rolls for minor violations. There I met many bright young people who were going to go on a similar downhill course as my friends a generation before. The economy was changing. And I worried about the implication for these children, their families, the African-American community, and society. What could be done to change the trajectory of their lives?

Gradually I began to understand that the difference between me and my hometown friends and these children was the quality of the developmental experience I received at home compared to theirs—through no fault of their parents. The parents, for historical and social reasons, were not able to adequately prepare their children for school.

I had to better understand all of the interacting forces. This led me to the School of Public Health at the University of Michigan, training in psychiatry at the Yale School of Medicine and eventually in child psychiatry at the Yale Child Study Center. The National Institute of Mental Health had paid for my training and they called me back to Washington, DC in 1968. That was one of the years of massive urban disturbances. Preparation of low-income minority children to participate in the mainstream of society was an important way to reduce social unrest. And yet the research proposals I was reviewing could not begin to touch the complexity of the problems, as I understood them.

My dream was to go out into the real world, and bring about school improvement at a level that would impact national thinking, practice, and policy. Before the year was over I received an invitation from Yale to direct a collaborative program between the Yale Child Study Center and the New Haven School System that was designed to improve schools for the children I was most concerned about.

We began with two of the lowest achieving, most troublesome elementary schools in the city. The usual focus at the time was on the students. But from my own experience and my public health and child psychiatry background I knew that we had to focus on the system and the child . . . not just the child. This was uncharted territory, but we knew that children develop and learn best through interactions with adults in safe and positive environments. The nine essential elements of the SDP emerged from the authentic effort to create these conditions. We began a process of applying theory to practice, evaluation, modification, refinement of theory, and then application of more refined theory to continuing and new challenges that were uncovered as change took place. Eventually, we became a national program.

The implication of the successes reported here and in many other places show that low-income children can gain the social and academic skills needed to do well in school and in life when the education enterprise adequately addresses their developmental needs. The authors point out that although our work began as an effort to help low-income, urban children, it has proved beneficial to students from all income groups; and rural, suburban, language, ethnic, and cultural groups. This is the case because all children must develop well to do well academically. Although some practitioners and policymakers are beginning to pay attention to the development students need to achieve well, too few do so.

Our hope now is to work in ways that will encourage many more practitioners and policymakers to "think development" and use the principles in their work. The case studies reported in *The Kids Got Smarter* will be most helpful in this regard. I am greatly appreciative of the work of the authors and their colleagues. And I thank the many parents, students, school and district staff who helped us learn; the colleges and universities who worked with us; my colleagues at Yale who supported a somewhat different approach to research and scholarship; the Rockefeller Foundation and many others, and particularly my colleague, Dr. Edward Joyner, whose education knowledge and skill enabled us to prepare people to use the SDP conceptual framework to bring about change; other SDP colleagues, and many others.

Series Preface

Books in this series, *Understanding Education and Policy*, will present a variety of perspectives to better understand the aims, practices, content and contexts of schooling, and the meaning of these analyses for educational policy. Our primary intent is to redirect the language used, the voices included in the conversation, and the range of issues addressed in the current debate concerning schools and policy. In doing this, books in the series will explore the differential conceptions and experiences that surface when analysis includes racial, class, gender, ethnic, and other key differences. Such a perspective will span the social sciences (anthropology, history, philosophy, psychology, sociology, etc.), and research paradigms.

Books in the series will be grounded in the contextualized lives of the major actors in school (students, teachers, administrators, parents, policy makers, etc.) and address major theoretical issues. The challenge to authors is to fully explore life-in-schools, through the multiple lenses of various actors and within the contexts in which these actors and schools are situated. It is anticipated that such a range of empirically sound and theoretically challenging work will contribute to a fundamental and needed rethinking of the content, process and context for school reform.

In *The Kids Got Smarter,* the authors examine schools that have been successful with a particular reform, James Comer's School Development Program (SDP). These studies detail the lived experience of urban schools that defy the assumption that urban schools serving disadvantaged students are bad schools. These schools are all excellent schools, and the School Development Program played a major role in these transformations. The studies also reveal that while the SDP is often assumed to be about improved services to children, it is a governance system as well. These schools used the more democratic process of the SDP to effect overall transformation. Nevertheless, as SDP itself advocates, it is not the reform, but what people do with the reform, that counts. This work challenges reformers who wish to market a "package" to demonstrate how the reform package promotes the necessary agency for school transformation. It is a fitting part of this book series.

Acknowledgments

We would like to thank the many people who made this research possible. The Rockefeller Foundation, and Jamie Jensen and Marla Ucelli in particular, initiated and funded the study. They facilitated the selection of schools and a productive relationship with the School Development Program at Yale University. Their comments on an earlier draft of this report led to a series of reanalyses of data and reinterpretations of the results of those data analyses. Beyond this they provided a supportive touchstone in times of uncertainty, of which this study afforded several. We also thank Barnett Berry for connecting us to the Foundation.

The School Development Program was also very supportive, helping with site selection and in educating the research team about the Comer Process. Norris Haynes was the initial colleague who assisted us with site selections and introductions to the schools. Norris also led us to other SDP staff—Joanne Corbin, Jack Gillett, and Valerie Maholmes, among others. We especially thank Ed Joyner for supporting our efforts early in the study and encouraging the schools to work with us. He also took our preliminary findings to heart and pushed us as well as his staff to think more about the wider implications of the case studies.

The schools and the people in them have pseudonyms in this volume, even though their accomplishments deserve widespread public recognition. The school principals, teachers, parents, community members, students, and others welcomed us, and took the risk of revealing themselves to us. They had faith they were doing good work that would tell its own story, and so it has. The research team maintained a critical perspective but to a person was impressed by the dedication and accomplishments of the people in these schools and communities.

We also thank Interim Dean William Burke of the School of Education at the University of North Carolina at Chapel Hill who saw this study as an example of the kinds of work our School should promote. He repeatedly interceded on our behalf in University procedures to insure this study would have the resources it needed.

Other people at UNC also made contributions to the project above and beyond the call of duty. Elizabeth Becker, an experiences researcher in her own right, stepped forward to produce the initial drafts. Catherine Awsumb edited and improved the case studies. Jean Patterson voluntarily took on many tasks that enabled the final draft to be ably and thoughtfully completed. Sharon Marlowe kept the project going in too many ways to enumerate. She literally took over the logistical details of the study to enable the research team to concentrate on the study. She also produced the final version, an amazing accomplishment given the number of authors and the time constraints involved. We thank Elizabeth, Catherine, and Sharon for saving us from ourselves.

1

Studying Successful Comer Schools

George W. Noblit
University of North Carolina at Chapel Hill

Paula R. Groves
University of North Carolina at Chapel Hill

Michael E. Jennings
Tufts University

Jean A. Patterson
Wichita State University

Jonathan Kozol, in *Savage Inequalities* (1991), portrayed the plight of urban schools in America. He documented the inadequate funding, dismal school buildings, and the harsh realities of life for poor children. He described demoralizing conditions, but also found educators who refused to be demoralized. These brave people all too often worked alone and found they had to try to ignore the terrible conditions in the rest of the school and community in order to stay committed. They persevered in spite of the schools.

Just as there are people who succeed despite the odds, there are also urban schools that succeed despite the odds. Our team of researchers had the opportunity to study five such schools. These schools were all "Comer schools"—schools that have implemented the School Development Program (SDP) designed by Dr. James Comer. They are successful schools that have committed faculties, involved parents, powerful leadership, and achieving students. The question that guided this research asked:

What was the role of the School Development Program (if any) in the success of these schools?

We learned that although the SDP was a vital part of the schools' success, it was but one contributing factor among many. The stories of these five successes reveal the complexity of creating successful urban schools.

In this book, we unravel this complexity to better understand the SDP as well as school reform. Yet we should not forget that the ultimate goal of reform is to improve the lives of children. In these successful Comer schools, we asked students to account for the changes at their schools. A girl at Gregory School (see Chapter 3) explained, as others nodded their heads, "the kids have gotten smarter." Although this is only part of the goal of improving the lives of children, this book is about accounting for how this belief was constructed. The stories of this construction in the five schools are as involved as they are compelling.

An understanding of the Comer initiative within the history of American schooling provides the backdrop for detailed case studies of the five schools, and a synthesis of the lessons from these schools. Our analysis complements Kozol's portrayal of the valor of educators, parents, and students. Consistent with Comer's approach, the significance of the SDP in these stories lies in the schools' creative application of the process.

THE SCHOOL DEVELOPMENT PROGRAM

In 1967 and 1968, researchers at the Yale Child Study Center sought to examine the problems of children who were being excluded from society's social and economic mainstream. They concluded that schools were the "natural" place to both help and study children (Comer, Haynes, & Joyner, 1996a; Comer, Haynes, Joyner, & Ben-Avie, 1996b). At this time, the Ford Foundation was actively supporting projects nationwide that utilized the resources of universities to support public education. Researchers from the Yale Child Study Center developed their program at the suggestion of Douglas Ferguson, a Project Officer with the Ford Foundation (Comer, 1993).

Dr. Albert Solnit, Director of the Yale Child Study Center, and Samuel Nash, Director of Special Projects for the New Haven School System, wrote a formal proposal to begin the study (Comer, 1993). The Ford Foundation accepted the proposal during the 1967-68 academic year. During this time, officials at Yale and with the New Haven Schools discussed and refined their conception of the study's guiding philosophy, methodology, and organization (Comer, 1993). Dr. Comer, who was completing his child psychiatry training in Washington, DC, returned to New Haven in 1968 to help direct the fledgling program. The basic premise of the program was that the application of the principles of social and behavioral science to every aspect of the school's program would improve the school's climate by fostering improved relationships among those involved with the school's operation. Additionally, researchers hoped that the application of these principles would foster a significant leap in the academic and social growth of the school's students (Comer, 1993).

Researchers selected Baldwin (K-6) and King (K-4) elementary schools in New Haven as the first research sites. Ninety-five percent of Baldwin's 360 students and King's 270 students were from lower and middle-income families. Student records revealed that 98% or more of the students in both schools were African American. Both schools reported low academic achievement, serious behavior problems, and poor attendance among their student bodies. Parents and staff at Baldwin and King suffered from low morale and were clearly frustrated with the conditions surrounding the school's existence (Comer, 1993).

Chaos and conflict characterized the program's first year in these two schools. Many parents were upset with the reform efforts, and many teachers were angry at what they felt was an attempt to blame them for the school's failures (Comer, 1993). Comer's team shunned the idea of entering the school with a prepackaged reform initiative "guaranteed" to cure the ills of the school. Instead, they attempted to learn, along with the school's teachers, how to best help the children (Comer et al., 1996a, 1996b). This effort resulted in the creation of a school-level approach to educational reform that would address the full spectrum of a school's operation (Comer et al., 1996a, 1996b).

Comer's team emphasized analyzing the school as a system in order to understand the complex interactions occurring within this system. Using paradigms from the fields of child psychiatry and public health, Comer designed the SDP to allow parents, teachers, administrators and staff to understand each others' needs and to then cooperate with one another in addressing those needs in an integrated and organized fashion (Comer et al., 1996a, 1996b). His early efforts forced Comer to realize that teachers, administrators, or parents rarely accept reform movements without opposition. Thus, Dr. Comer sought to promote change by encouraging families and staff to:

> engage in a process in which they gain knowledge of systems, of child development, and of individual behavior and apply it to every aspect of school programs in a way and at a rate that is understandable and non-threatening. When faithfully adhered to from the start, these mechanisms help the people involved achieve the kinds of small early successes critical to reinforcing confidence in the new program. (Comer et al., 1996a, p. 8)

To achieve these goals, the SDP organizes the school community (i.e., all persons working with the school and those living in the community) into three teams that together form the foundation of the program: the School Planning and Management Team (SPMT), the Parent Team (PT), and the Student and Staff Support Team (SSST). These three teams, referred to as the *three mechanisms*, guide the decision making of the SDP and ensure that all members of the school community have input into the decision-making process. The three guiding principles of *consensus, collaboration,* and *no fault* shape the decisions that drive these three mechanisms.

The concept of *consensus* discourages the idea of voting on particular issues of concern. Comer felt that voting on specific issues leads to a "zero-sum" game in which there are clearly defined "winners" and "losers" in the school's decision-making bodies. Instead, the principle of consensus urges all concerned to work toward an agreed outcome/solution that is acceptable to everyone.

Collaboration encourages inclusion and respect among all members of the school community. Achieving collaboration requires that parents, teachers, administrators, and others involved in the process respect others' points of view. This respect in turn facilitates a willingness to work cooperatively in pursuit of common goals.

The last of the guiding principles involves the concept of n*o fault* decision making. This principle discourages the assignment of blame for the problems within any given school and requires the examination of problems from such a viewpoint that everyone shares equal responsibility for positive change. This atmosphere of shared responsibility fosters a positive environment in which the best interests of the children remain the primary concern of the entire school community.

The primary mechanism of the SDP is the School Planning and Management Team (SPMT). The SPMT coordinates all school activities and is the school's central organizing committee. Usually led by the principal, the SPMT comprises parents, teachers, and staff. Its purpose is to balance input and representation from the entire school community. The major function of the SPMT is to create and implement a Comprehensive School Plan that reflects the goals of the school community in terms of academics, social climate and staff development. The SPMT develops and coordinates specific programs to aid in the accomplishment of these goals. Furthermore, the SPMT assesses and monitors the entire process of change in the school and then makes needed adjustments to ensure proper SDP implementation (Comer et al., 1996a, 1996b). This consistent effort to empower local school communities has been the hallmark of the SDP's effort to ensure that all of its actions are in the best interests of the students (Comer et al., 1996a, 1996b).

The Parent Team (PT) seeks to involve parents at every level of school life in order to foster a stronger link between home and school. At the most basic level, parents participate in support activities such as the Parent Teacher Association (PTA) and attend other school activities and social events. At the second level, parents are physically present in the schools, serving as volunteers or paid assistants in classrooms, libraries, cafeterias, or in other rooms as needed. At the third level, parents select other parents to be representatives on the SPMT. As members of the SPMT, they are able to convey the feelings and opinions of parents on a variety of topics that affect the school community. The PT is an important aspect of the SDP because it empowers parents through participation in the school-wide decision-making process. The PT also serves to bridge the often large cultural/socioeconomic gap between home and school that can lead to problems for some "disadvantaged" students (Comer et al., 1996a, 1996b).

The Student and Staff Support Team (SSST) addresses both macro- and micro-level issues dealing with school climate and the psychosocial development of the students. The SSST includes staff, professionals, child development, and mental health professionals. These include the guidance counselor, school psychologist, school nurse, speech therapist, truant officer, and any other professionals deemed appropriate. The SSST attempts to work "preventively and prescriptively" in addressing the concerns of individual students and the school community as a whole. The SSST helps design and implement interventions for individual students. On a school-wide level, the SSST seeks to confront community-wide and society-wide issues that affect student development. By confronting these issues on both an individual and a school-wide basis, the SSST works to prevent crises from occurring rather than simply reacting to crises that have already developed (Comer et al., 1996a, 1996b).

Central to the functioning of these three mechanisms is an emphasis on understanding child development. Comer recognized early on that dissonance between school and home would adversely affect student behavior and academic achievement. He felt that the key to reducing this dissonance was to emphasize the proper development of the individual child. Thus, child development is a central component of the Comer Process. Comer emphasized six aspects of child development (which he labeled as *developmental pathways*) that, if properly emphasized, would ensure that all children learn and develop to their fullest potential. Comer assures us that:

> For a student to arrive on the school's doorstep adequately prepared to learn and behave well at five years of age, the caretakers (usually parents) and others in the child's environment should have stimulated early development along important developmental lines. . . . (Comer, 1993, p. 31)

The six developmental pathways are the physical, cognitive, psychological, language, social, and ethical dimensions of child development. Because each of these dimensions is equally important, Comer emphasizes that the dimensions must be balanced for each child to reach his or her fullest potential. Balanced development (i.e., "maturity") results from proper linkage between the pathways. Overemphasizing or underemphasizing any of the six individual pathways results in unbalanced development.

The SDP has grown tremendously since its inception in 1968 and has evolved through three stages. The first stage lasted from 1968 to 1978 and began with the use of the SDP in two elementary schools in New Haven, Connecticut. These pilot programs included further development and refinement of the SDP design. The second stage extended from 1978 to 1988 and involved testing the SDP in Prince George's County, Maryland; Norfolk, Virginia; Benton, Michigan; and several other schools in New Haven, Connecticut. Researchers provided training to personnel from school districts and individual schools to implement the SDP. Researchers also began to test the effectiveness of the program in various schools. Results of these studies showed that when faithfully implemented, the SDP indeed had positive effects on school climate which then correlated with positive student outcomes (Emmons, Owen, Haynes, & Comer, 1992; Haynes & Bility, 1994). The third SDP stage, largely supported by the Rockefeller Foundation, began in 1988 and extends to the present. During this stage, program developers have focused on developing new strategies for nation-wide dissemination of the SDP.

This third stage of SDP also saw the creation of a training program known as the Comer Project for Change in Education (CPCE), the goal of which was to aid school districts in sustained implementation of the SDP through a "trainer-of-trainers of model" (Comer et al., 1996a, p. 21). Other newly developed programs emphasizing implementation include: the development of partnerships with schools of education that orient pre-service teachers to SDP strategies; the use of Regional Professional Development Centers (RPDCs) to support the implementation of SDPs in specific geographical areas; the Systemic Implementation (SI) initiative that infuses SDP principles at the district level to ensure continued support by district administrators who oversee individual schools; and the Comer-Zigler (Co-Zi) project that brings together family and community services in an effort to prepare preschool age children for school (Comer et al., 1996a, 1996b).

A PERSPECTIVE ON EDUCATION, RACE AND REFORM

There are least two histories of American education. One history is of progress and uplift in which schools function as great equalizers for our democracy as well as engines for economic development. In this history, schools may stratify their students as part of a meritocracy, but all students may still demonstrate merit and receive the appropriate rewards. A second history is less optimistic. According to this history, the goals of schools were to preserve the culture of the early settlers, to control the influx of new immigrants and their cultural and religious beliefs, and to convert them into workers for the newly emerging industrial economy. Schools were to reproduce a dominant culture and economic system. In short, both histories of education are true, if partial, accounts of how schools work for both whites and people of color. Schools are vehicles for social mobility as well as deniers of opportunity. Many students, especially those of the dominant culture, flourish in schools and use the knowledge gained in them for professional and social growth. These students are mostly white Americans. People of color have repeatedly demonstrated their faith in education (Anderson, 1988), as they created educational opportunities for themselves during conditions of slavery and segregation. Emancipation, religion, and education were linked in their struggles for freedom and equality. During segregation, Washington (1965) and DuBois (1935), respectively, recast the two histories of education as strategies for pursuing equality. Nonetheless, with desegregation, African Americans lost control of their schools and found themselves subject to a caste-like status system (Ogbu, 1978, 1995). Schools purported to provide equality of opportunity, but in practice, the two histories of education bifurcated by race. For whites, schools were likely to provide opportunities for social mobility. For African Americans, schools were likely to deny opportunity. Moreover, desegregation undercut African American communities, thus separating education from emancipation and racial uplift (Dempsey & Noblit, 1995; Noblit & Dempsey, 1996; Siddle Walker, 1993). As Shujaa (1994) phrased it, for African Americans there has been too much schooling and too little education.

Ogbu (1978, 1995) and others have shown that the experience with schools for other people of color who were "involuntary immigrants," including Latinos and Native Americans, was similar to that of African Americans. Whereas "voluntary" immigrants of color at first believed American schools to be much as the first history of education portrays it (especially as it compares with education in their home nations), succeeding generations of these same immigrants, as well as poor whites and people of color, experienced the second history of education. Their history of education is not that of progress and mobility, but of stratification and denial of opportunity.

Americans are notably ahistorical in their understanding of social and educational change (Sarason, 1997). This ahistoricity has predictable consequences. With this focus on the present, Americans forget that educational reform has a history dating at least to antiquity (Kimball 1986). Sarason (1997) argues that presentism interacts with a second propensity to treat what is the "barometer" of change as change itself. Thus, educational reformers misconstrue symptoms and the effects of change, rather than understand what was, in fact, the change. Americans tend to argue that change can be controlled and managed. They confuse instrumental rationality with substantive rationality (Collins, 1982). Americans address change by rational processes of planning and organizational structures but tend to neglect the values and goals that are the content of change. Finally, there is a tendency to view change itself as good, without any consideration of the substance of change. The result is that public schools often become the pawns of change instead of participants in deliberating its substance, direction, and meaning (Noblit & Dempsey, 1996). Recent educational reformers seem to be prime examples of the preceding scenario. They all too often forget history, focus on symptoms, assume rationality, and want pawns to implement the change others value. Educational reforms often "tightly couple" (Weick, 1976, p. 3) schools, centralizing authority and constructing justifications for both the need and substance of reform.

Most analysts believe that the current reform era began in 1983 with the publication of *A Nation at Risk*. The National Commission on Excellence in Education (1983) argued that slipping economic competitiveness could be laid at the feet of educators in what was regarded as a "rising tide of mediocrity" (p. 5). This report and those that followed accepted the idea that education was in crisis and "something must be done." Business leaders, the media, and the government set the agenda, which included setting aside the concern with equity prompted by school desegregation. These same organizations then created a new role for state government that displaced educators in the policymaking arena. The state and the business community also used a new set of policy tools to influence the "turn to excellence." "High stakes" testing set the new accountability policy in place and set in motion efforts by schools and districts to align instruction with curricula and testing. Thus, states began to affect the internal operations of schools in ways they had not before. The new state and business roles in the "waves" of reform in the 1980s led to new understanding about reform and changes in the logic of reform. (Murphy, 1990; Zeichner, 1991).

Analysts characterize the first wave of reform that followed *A Nation at Risk* as being about increasing centralization of schools at the state level, using a bureaucratic model of change, and devising prescriptive policies that included accountability testing. Many commentators assumed that poor student outcomes were due to inadequate teaching and curricula and that educators had proven themselves inadequate to the task of improving schools. Reform reports proliferated, each adding new proposals to the mix of reforms (Murphy, 1990). In general, these reforms attempted to "tighten up the system." They called for more requirements, more supervision, more time on instruction, and so on. The first wave of reform, of course, left the structure of schools unchanged and, even worse, more tightly coupled than ever. Reformers then began to move into a second wave of reforms (1986-89) designed to restructure schools, but they did not reconsider the reforms of the first wave. They left the more centralized system in place as they moved on to consider teacher professionalization and site-based management. The efforts at decentralization, of course, were to take place within the centralization of the first-wave reforms. This context largely defeated the decentralization efforts even as the rhetoric claimed the goals were actually parental choice, empowerment, and fundamental restructuring.

The third reform wave began in the late 1980s with the recognition of the incompatibility of first- and second-wave reforms. Analysts argued that previous reforms had missed two central problems: the separation of schools and families; and the need to develop, beyond existing policy goals, the cognitive *capabilities* of young people (Hawley, 1988). Consequently, wave-three reforms focused on interagency collaboration and integrated services to young people. Wave-three reformers believed schools could become a central part of a new system of services geared to better serve the needs of children and youth. Adkins, Awsumb, Noblit, and Richards (1999) argued that the focus on children was heartening but also justified by an efficiency logic. The goals were not only to serve youth better, but cheaper. Unfortunately, collaboration proved to be much more difficult than originally thought and to require increased resources devoted to collaboration itself. It is also true that clients have a mixed view of such efforts. While in favor of better services, they also worry about the intrusion and control this affords government agencies.

It is difficult to assess the effects of these reforms, but Fiske (1991) argues that close examination of the impact of these reforms will lead one to conclude: "There *weren't* any" (p. 24, emphasis in original). Fiske argues the reason for this was simply that these reforms did not contain any new ideas about education. Warren (1990) agrees with Fiske but also adds: "Educational reform has tended to arise from perceived failures of schools to serve certain social goals adequately. Rarely has it affirmed education as intrinsically valuable" (p. 76).

Although these assessments of reform may seem harsh, there are other analyses that are more devastating, even as they offer an explanation for the failure of reform. Berliner and Biddle (1997) and Bracey (1997) have argued that the recent reform era was marshaled on top of a false crisis. Systematically they demonstrate that there was no crisis and that schools and achievement have had steady gains. They conclude that enemies of the public schools initiated the reform era. Historians of education (Cuban, 1988; Kent, 1987; Tyack, Lowe, & Hansot, 1984) also recount the recycling of reform in this century, including the waves of our recent reform era. Cuban sees "the inevitable return of school reforms" (1990, p. 3) as due, not to the failings of schools or of reform initiatives, but to "conflicts over values" (p. 7). He argues that reform recycles because value shifts in the larger society lead the schools to accommodate, or to adjust, rather than fundamentally change. The implementation of reforms limits the same value conflicts that stimulate reform. The recycling pattern helps perpetuate the value conflict by periodically recreating perceived "crises" in education.

Further, the waves of reforms sponsored by state and local governments that followed the publication of *A Nation at Risk* show remarkable ignorance of the second history of education, described earlier in this chapter. These reformers assumed the first history of education, arguing that increasing standards would naturally result in increased educational attainment. They "forgot" that the second history is also in play in schools that serve the poor. Asserting the first history does not make it real for the poor, and, in fact, may highlight the differences in how schools serve the poor and the more well-to-do. James Comer understood the second history of education, and the differences in how schools served the poor and the more well-to-do. Fifteen years before *A Nation at Risk,* Comer embarked on his own reform effort.

As a proponent of equity, the SDP is in direct contrast to the centralization of the first wave of 1980s reform. Although the SDP often has strong district support, usually in the form of training, in operation it is a school-based reform. Instead of tightly coupling the school to state reform and district mandate, the Comer Process focuses more on *horizontal* tight coupling. That is, the SDP integrates the various aspects of school work into more of a system. A democratically derived comprehensive school plan links three mechanisms. Staff make decisions in accordance with the three principles of no fault, consensus, and collaboration, and a focus on what is developmentally appropriate for the children. The school plan, of course, may well respond to the external mandates of the state created during the first wave of reform but, as we discuss later, in doing so transforms external accountability into a form of internal accountability. With SDP, schools respond to external accountability policy less as a form of compliance and more out of consideration for what is good for the children.

The SDP has more similarities with the second and third waves of reform than the first. With a representative governance system and a focus on children, the Comer Process offers much of what the second wave of reform promoted but did not deliver. Similarly, the SDP's focus on community and integrated services (through the SSST) is quite consistent with the third wave's emphases. These similarities with the second and third waves of reform may in part be responsible for the popularity of the SDP, but the waves are neither the genesis nor the reason for the SDP.

The SDP has implications for much more than the simple reform of schools. It is part of a larger struggle for the values that education will serve. There is little doubt that the SDP promotes equity. Further, the SDP explicitly addresses urban schools-largely ignored in the recent reform era and seemingly intractable to any reform era in this century-in part because urban school reform seems to require the reform and restructuring of cities themselves (Anyon, 1997).

Even though the SDP emerges from a different history than the recent reform era and is more about equity than excellence, recent research on successful reform efforts validate the Comer Process. According to a number of authors (Beck & Murphy, 1996; Goens & Clover, 1991; Sergiovanni, 1987), schools that have successfully reformed seem to have: (a) a sense of ownership; (b) an increased focus on the school community itself; (c) a new sense of shared responsibility for the welfare of the students; (d) a comprehensive view of education that goes beyond standardized testing to include relationships and ethics; and (e) a set of shared characteristics. For Goens and Clover (1991), the components of successful school reform include attention given to culture, leadership, quality, climate, outcomes, and productivity. Beck and Murphy (1996) argue there are "four imperatives" in successful schools: (a) a focus on promoting learning; (b) strong and facilitative leadership; (c) cultivating a sense of community within the school and between the school and its external community; and (d) support for staff and parents to promote improved student achievement. Although these lists are different in number and terminology, the substance being discussed is quite similar.

The SDP has emphasized many of the same things these studies of successfully reformed schools identify as important. The SDP both asks schools to choose to become a Comer school and uses its training, the developmental pathway mechanisms, principles, and the comprehensive school plan to promote ownership, a focus on the school community, a sense of shared responsibility, a comprehensive view of education, and a similar set of school characteristics of education. Moreover, the SDP's emphasis on schools being "data driven" causes schools to consider and reflect on productivity and outcomes. In short, although the SDP emerges from a different history, its ideas and processes seem to reflect what the recent reform era has learned about successfully reforming schools. Comer's design and the SDP training for Comer schools focus on what research suggests is necessary for schools to change and improve.

DOES THE SDP MAKE A DIFFERENCE?

Although initially designed as a process to make schools more responsive to the needs of low (SES) African American students, the SDP has evolved into an inclusive effort for diversity in general. Findings from our research indicate that the SDP is a process that embraces all issues of diversity. Language-different, special education, affluent, and low achieving majority students exhibit positive social adjustment and respectable academic achievement with the SDP. With the focus on "what is best for the child," the SDP does not prescribe a particular instructional method or curricular modification, and instead favors a variety of pedagogical approaches. Driven by this perspective, the schools in this study tended to develop educational strategies for inclusion rather than develop a rationale for exclusion.

The fact that over 640 schools have now implemented the Comer Process provides testimony that many people believe that it speaks to their situation and promises to allow them to improve their schools. Moreover, it is clear that schools that have implemented the SDP have experienced gains in achievement (Comer, 1988). In a number of districts, in addition to significant gains in achievement, Comer schools report increased attendance, reduction in punishments for student misbehavior, improved student attitudes and self-concept, and more positive assessments of school climate (Comer & Haynes, 1992). All of these are impressive accomplishments, but they are aggregate effects. In short, many of these studies assume that because schools implemented SDP the improved results are in fact due to the SDP. Reformers and researchers desired an assessment of how SDP is implicated in such successful results and how it is not. We designed this study in cooperation with the Rockefeller Foundation to discover and analyze what connections, if any, were evident between the SDP and school success. We studied five schools that had implemented the Comer Process and had positive changes in student achievement, discipline, and parent involvement to document what connections existed between the SDP and school success.

CASE STUDY DESIGN

Our research used a descriptive and interpretive format to tell the stories of the SDP in five schools, and a comparative design to synthesize the meanings of a set of case studies for the SDP and for educational reform in general. This comparative design required that we gather similar data in all the sites and that each case study address similar issues, but not necessarily in the same ways or order. Thus, we preserved the uniqueness of the schools while also synthesizing lessons from the set. A biracial research team (Co-PI and one research assistant) assumed responsibility for each school. Team composition was appropriate to the schools studied, to our own commitments, and to understanding the multiple perspectives. This allowed the teams to gather fuller data because different investigators see somewhat different things, and the ensuing dialogue over these perceptions was a vital part of coming to an adequate understanding of each case.

Site Selection

The School Development Program nominated 37 of the existing 640 Comer Schools for inclusion in this study. We then narrowed this list to 11 schools that met the selection criteria of: (a) being at least three years into the implementation of the SDP; (b) showing evidence of a positive trajectory in student achievement, discipline, and parent involvement; (c) being inclusive of all grade levels of schooling; and (d) being located in different regions of the United States. In subsequent discussions, we narrowed the list to five schools: three elementary (one was K-8) schools, one middle school, and one high school. The schools were geographically varied (south, north, and west) and had somewhat differing student populations (multiethnic, Asian-African-American, African-American-Latino, and African-American-Anglo). To preserve anonymity, pseudonyms have been used for all schools and people.

There was one possible departure from the selection criteria. The school district of the middle school nominated for the study explained that the school was undergoing a set of transitions that made it a poor choice for our purposes. They proposed a replacement that was in the second year of SDP implementation, but which they argued had already achieved a high level of implementation and had improved on the dimensions of success required for this study. Thus, we included Trivette Middle School in the study.

Team Training

Although the research team was very experienced in case study research and had worked together in a variety of ways, it was still necessary to spend the beginning weeks of the project exploring the SDP, developing data collection strategies and instruments, deciding how to handle difficult situations, and deciding how to explain our project to people on site. Two team members observed an SDP training session in New Haven, Connecticut, in order to gain a better understanding of the SDP. Three team members spent a day visiting a local Comer school (not selected for the study) to familiarize themselves with how the SDP functioned on a daily basis. The team held weekly meetings throughout the study to reinforce this initial training, to adapt to changes in the research plan and/or understanding of the project, and to insure the accomplishment of each task.

Methodology

Descriptive and interpretive case studies typically use observation, interviewing, and document review as the major data collection techniques. We systematically conducted observations of classrooms, the three types of Comer team meetings, teacher planning periods, PTA/O meetings, and the school and community. We toured the schools and communities and attended all possible PTO and other parent and/or community meetings related to school functions. The goals of the observations were: (a) to depict the everyday life in the schools and their communities; (b) to understand the specific mechanisms the school employed to achieve its successes; and (c) to ascertain how the SDP played into both the everyday life of the schools and their communities and into the production of school successes.

We used individual and focus-group interviews as a primary data collection technique to elicit the multiple perspectives that people held about education, the school, and the SDP. These interviews contributed to an understanding of the schools' implementation of the Comer Process in view of its situational dynamics, instructional school context, and social scenes. It should be noted that schools such as those studied here have had a great deal of public exposure and as such have a practiced image that they portray. The research team took great pains to get beyond the surface characterizations by seeking out people who previously had not talked, asking for corroborating data, and delving beneath surface explanations. For example, many of the schools insisted that there were no "cliques," which prompted each team to interrogate interviewees immediately. Further, when we noted that all five schools shared this portrayal, we designed site visits, in part, to see if disconfirming evidence could be generated. As a result, we established that the schools did have teacher networks but that the interviewees had been correct; networks were more affiliational than political. Teachers had friendship groups but were essentially united in their support of the SDP and the school.

The schools provided some documentary data to the research team, including data on student achievement, attendance, redistricting, family mobility, demographics, and the school improvement efforts underway at each of the schools. We gathered redistricting, mobility, and demography data to illustrate those contextual conditions over which schools have little influence. The documentary data on the various school improvement efforts, both current and in recent history, were essential for understanding exactly what was proposed and what was in fact accomplished. We collected every applicable document available at these schools, including curricula, school and district reports, grant proposals, memos, meeting minutes, PTO documents, newsletters, program reviews, evaluations of programs, and accreditation reports. These data allowed a fuller understanding of all that the school had undertaken and what the results have been. They also allowed for an understanding of competing and/or complementary initiatives, as well as how school officials represented the initiatives to various publics.

Each two-person team spent a total of 70 person-days on site to gather data that were detailed, reflected multiple perspectives, tracked organizational processes, and depicted each school's culture, micropolitics, and environments. Repeated site visits allowed us to crosscheck data, follow leads, document patterns, and confirm interpretations.

Data Collection and Instruments

First site visit. We conducted individual interviews with representatives from the school district administration, the school principal and vice-principals, counselors, and community representatives. We conducted focus-group interviews with students, parents and teachers, and we observed Comer team meetings and used a portion of the meeting for a focus-group interview. During these interviews we attempted to address all the research questions and sections of the case profile. We observed classrooms selected for variety in teaching approaches. These classes included academic, fine arts, and those for gifted, remedial, and exceptional children. We spent four person-days at each of the initial five schools. This broad-gauged approach was necessary given the time frame available for data collection.

Preliminary data analysis. The case profile just discussed also served as the format for the case record of each school (Merriam, 1988). Immediately after returning from the field, the site visit team developed case records for each school that followed the case-profile categories. These records allowed a preliminary assessment of the key themes/issues/tropes that characterized each school's story, additional data and interviews needed, and development of a site-specific plan for more focused inquiry during the second site visit. For each site, the team developed a preliminary analysis of the system and system-like connections between the SDP and the school's success.

Second site visits. The purpose of the second site visits was to gather the needed data identified in the preliminary data analysis and to begin focused inquiries into the multiple perspectives on the school's success and the role of the SDP in that success. Each of the schools had a specific data-collection plan that enabled data to yield a complete case profile and an interpretation of the meaning of the Comer Process in the school's success. Again, each team spent four person-days in each school.

Case records. After the second site visits, the research teams developed complete case records on each of the four schools. These records allowed us to interpret the role of the SDP in each school's success, which in essence yielded the "story" of each school. These stories were, of course, tentative for key data; we triangulated and thus confirmed, modified, and/or rejected each interpretation. We also identified alternative explanations.

Third site visits. Our emphases for the third site visits were on triangulating data and interpretations and exploring alternative explanations for the data previously collected. We asked on-site people who had been helpful informants to respond to our understandings of the school, its success, and the role of the SDP in the school's success. These "member checks" (Patton, 1990) were important sources of information for determining how to best represent the school's story. At this stage, we devoted at least two person-days to each school. At each school, the Co-PI and research assistant conducted an exit debriefing with a group of representatives of the various stakeholders of the SDP and school. This debriefing served as a form of triangulation in itself, but it also served to reduce the anticipation and/or surprises that the written draft case studies could have provoked. These debriefing sessions also provided an opportunity for dialogue among the school staffs as a means of "phenomenon recognition," during which the researchers' present their sense of reality to those who live the reality and are in a position to judge the researchers' interpretations of the data.

Fourth site visits. After we completed a draft of the cases and the final report in Fall 1997, we sent a copy to each school for review and critique. The two-person research team for each school returned for one day to discuss the draft with school staff. These visits provided additional data, and we detected no substantive flaws in the cases.

Data Analysis

The research team initially analyzed the data as they collected it. Over the summer of 1997, we categorized data using Miles and Huberman's (1994) matrix approach to qualitative analysis. We arrayed data into categories that the study was designed to assess and the themes that were identified in the ongoing data analyses. We also conducted a more inductive, constant, comparative method (Glaser & Strauss, 1967) of analysis to determine if this process generated a different set of themes and understandings of the school and the relationship of the SDP to the school's apparent success.

We compared the themes that emerged from the latter process to those that emerged during the Spring data collection; this comparison served as another form of triangulation for the case studies and yielded a final interpretation for each case. We compared and synthesized the school-by-school interpretations to acknowledge the schools' uniquenesses, as well as their similarities. We derived lessons from these comparisons to inform policymakers and educators interested in the SDP and reform in general. According to Noblit and Hare (1988), case study comparisons entail translations of one case into the others. Our first step was to identify the key themes, tropes, and metaphors for each case. Then, we constructed a matrix that allowed us to compare those themes, tropes, and metaphors. A set of cross-site themes resulted that accounted for both the diversity and similarity among the cases. Finally, we synthesized the data into a composite heuristic model depicting the connections between key features of the school, the SDP, and student achievement.

The draft report contained all these analyses. The schools reviewed and responded to their own cases. Representatives from the SDP and the Rockefeller Foundation read the full draft report and offered helpful critiques and suggestions. The research team carefully considered this feedback, and we have incorporated the responses and suggestions received into this book.

THIS BOOK

Merriam (1988) notes that case studies can be descriptive, interpretive, or evaluative. This report is descriptive and interpretive rather than evaluative and cannot be seen as an adequate evaluation of the SDP. However, it is a rigorous examination of how context effects the systemic qualities of the SDP. Such a study illuminates the prospects of the SDP in various contexts and can offer lessons about the meaning of school contexts to the SDP itself. Although we do not determine if the SDP is a meritorious innovation (House, 1977), we describe the connections of the SDP to indicators of school success and interpret the meanings of the SDP in the schools studied.

The next section of this book contains the full case study for each school. These case studies, while presenting each school's unique story, describe how the SDP is defined, practiced, and related to the school's success. A cross-site analysis follows the case studies. In this analysis, we compare and synthesize the stories in order to determine what they reveal about the SDP and educational reform. In the conclusion, we present a graphic representation of how the SDP is embedded in the schools and how it contributes to success in these five schools. We conclude by offering a set of implications of this study for the SDP and for educational reform writ large.

2

Oceanview Elementary School

Paula R. Groves
University of North Carolina at Chapel Hill

"Basket! Happy! Sunny! Trees!", a Somali first grader dressed in a red cape blurts while skipping on the center rug. A Vietnamese student sits erect at a desk carefully and diligently outlining the letters of the English alphabet with a big green crayon while a teaching assistant completes the same worksheet by his side. In the "Imagination Corner," three children of differing cultures play house together with a makeshift kitchen. With the soft blow of a train whistle all the children switch positions and rotate in groups to begin another activity.

This is a typical 30-minute block of the first and second grade newcomer class at Oceanview Elementary School. This class is some children's first experience in a classroom or school setting. It is the first place they have learned to pick up a pencil, use paper, or sit at a desk in a plastic chair. It is the first experience the children have in which they are taught to speak and understand the English language. To blurt out words in English while acting out a scene from "Little Red Riding Hood" is an exciting accomplishment, a sign that they are learning, understanding, and getting accustomed to their foreign environment.

The class consists of 20 students of differing cultures, religions, and backgrounds, all recent immigrants with limited English skills. But, despite what might seem to be a language barrier, learning takes place, and the children find ways to communicate with each other and the teacher. The teacher's gentle and caring teaching style lets the children know that they are the center of his agenda and that he is there to support their development and ease the socialization process. Somali, Vietnamese, and Cambodian teaching assistants float in and out of the class to provide comfort and to aid in translations as needed.

17

Nurturing classroom environments, multicultural and multilingual students, and a supportive teaching staff are not limited to this particular newcomer class. They are all elements that permeate the school, components of the school's culture that are responsible for much of the school's success.

The ethnic diversity of Oceanview Elementary School is a direct reflection of the school's immediate neighborhood. As a neighborhood school, Oceanview houses the 1,350 students who live within a 9-block boundary. The neighborhood is characterized by high mobility and an amazing diversity of languages. New immigrants and low-income groups are constantly moving in and out of the inexpensive housing in the area. Within just the 9-block neighborhood boundary of the school, over 37 different languages and dialects are spoken.

Over the past 16 years, most of the families moving in have been Vietnamese, Cambodian, Laotian, African, and Hispanic. Immigrant populations settle into this particular neighborhood primarily because of the low rent and the fact that there are many rental homes as well as apartments. More than 31% of the residents in the community have incomes under $15,000, with 24% having incomes under $10,000. Whereas some immigrant populations have not stayed very long, like the Polish and Estonians who used the area as a stepping stone before moving to other areas, the Asian, African, and Hispanic populations do not appear to be moving away. As the district nurse describes the neighborhood from which Oceanview draws its students:

> The community is a high need community; we are about 98% Aid to Families of Dependent Children (AFDC). We have a large group from Somalia, a large group from Kenya, Ethiopia and other parts of Africa from refugee camps. I have just received children from Tahiti who had a horrendous story to tell me. We have had the flow of the Cambodian and Vietnamese and now we are over 50% Hispanic, many who are undocumented immigrants that have just crossed the border. The legal immigrants come from war torn countries. For many refugees, this is their first exposure in the United States with their children entering the schools.

Because of the ethnic diversity and various economic needs of the neighborhood, Oceanview has become a multifaceted community resource, supportive of residents' cultures and helping them adjust to their new environment. The school, however, cannot address all of the community's problems. Cultural differences, linguistic misunderstandings, and a fight for scarce resources in an extremely overcrowded and impoverished area lead to problems that transcend the limits of the school. The neighborhood is plagued with conflict between and within ethnic groups that has translated into crime and gang violence.

Because of the ever-changing context of the community, Oceanview has historically had to adapt to the multicultural populations of students entering and exiting the school. Annual student turnover/mobility rates for the cluster of schools serving the area have been as high as 120%. In 1996, 72.8% of

Oceanview's student body was stable, but this appearance of stability masks a constant stream of entries and exits. In the same year, 1,059 new students were registered; that is, one third of the student population turned over three times. As one administrator described the school's history and demographics:

> This was one of the early schools built in the school district. Since that time it has gone through a number of changes. It used to be pretty middle class dominant and it used to be predominantly white. Through the years it has changed and become a low-income area with a lot of ethnic diversity. This was one of the first places the Vietnamese settled when the large immigration occurred in the late 70s and early 80s. At that time the school was predominantly South East Asian, African-American and White. Since then, there has been a continuing growth of the Latino population. We are now 67 percent Latino. It was then that the Cambodian population also immigrated and established first roots. So now there has been a new wave of immigration of the Somali population. It is hard to know what is African and what is African-American because the coding is the same. So when you look at that statistic it says African-American about 16 percent, but a big chunk of that is the Somali population.

Clearly, Oceanview faces enormous and ongoing challenges in adapting its program to meet the constantly changing needs of their students and community. This case study depicts how the Comer School Development Process (SDP) has provided Oceanview with a governance structure and guiding philosophy that facilitates such responsiveness. Section II describes the school's attraction to Comer as a mechanism for responding productively to change. Section III details the successes the school has achieved since implementing Comer. Section IV describes reform initiatives adopted by Oceanview in tandem with Comer as part of the overall emphasis on meeting the needs of the whole child. Section V provides details on the structure and vision of the Comer SDP as implemented at Oceanview. Section VI discusses the school's attempts to implement Comer principles at the classroom level. Section VII concludes by outlining Oceanview's vision for the future of the SDP at the school.

THE COMER PROCESS AS A MECHANISM FOR RESPONDING TO RAPIDLY CHANGING STUDENT NEEDS

It was not until a few years ago, with a new administrator and the adoption of the Comer model, that many people felt the school began to evolve to support the changing needs of the community. The restructuring of the school with the Comer model translated into a change, not only in the school's climate and guiding principles, but in the teaching staff and instructional program as well. In terms of climate, Oceanview staff and administration saw a shift from an environment focusing on order and control to a more inviting and "parent friendly" environment. More tangibly, Comer's emphasis on data-driven analysis of how to meet student needs led to a change in instructional programming and staffing. In its examination of student needs, Oceanview realized that even though the student population radically changed, the faculty was still mostly composed of Anglo teachers who taught courses in English to students who barely spoke the language. To address this mismatch, bilingual teachers were added and the number of bilingual classrooms was doubled so that children were no longer misplaced in regular classrooms. Teaching assistants who represented the different cultures of the school were added to help in classrooms and with translations at parent events.

With over 75% of students classified as Limited English Proficient (LEP) and 85% as English Language Learners (ELL), Oceanview now consists of mostly bilingual and "sheltered" classrooms. The numbers of these classes have ballooned since the adoption of the Comer Process, as they were identified as one of the many changes needed to appropriately serve the needs of the students. Oceanview currently has 26 bilingual classes conducted in Spanish, three transition classes, and 18 sheltered classes composed of students speaking a variety of languages. Two of the sheltered classes are designated as "newcomer" classes for the 5% of the student population who have been in the United States for less than one year.

Principal Amanda Scythe's perspective is that "stability for the stake of stability isn't always good" and that the changes the school underwent were all positive. But, as with any major reform, the school encountered tensions. For some, the huge cultural change felt "like a freight train" coming through the school. The change in teaching staff, which resulted in many new and inexperienced teachers, required teacher training to become a priority among the many other changes.

Despite these inevitable tensions, teachers and administrators alike agreed that change was necessary and that the school had plenty of room for improvement. Within the first few months of assuming her position as the schools' new principal, Amanda Scythe decided that Comer would be the most fruitful reform path for the school. She pointed to a number of reasons why the Comer Process is a good fit with Oceanview's needs:

> One was the successes that had been demonstrated by the Comer program [in] the way it addressed issues of poverty. Second, there weren't any parents around in the school. There were personnel who worked for parent groups and what they kept telling me was that we can't get the parents involved. That didn't read right. So it felt to me like, I knew the achievement of the school had been declining, our standardized test scores had been consistently declining and had reached what looked like to me as crisis proportions. So it was helpful for me to say the achievement is not where it needs to be, and the School Development Program is a program

that has had a track record of improving achievement. I heard the teachers and staff saying if we had more parents involved we could be better. In my point of view I used those things as leverages in order to sell the notion of Comer communication.

With the constantly changing population of children attending the school, and the growing numbers of students from multicultural and multilingual backgrounds, Ms. Scythe believed that the ideologies and principles of Comer could help the school keep in sync with evolving student and community needs. The school has always had a very dedicated staff and administration that cared for the students and made countless efforts to involve the students' parents and families. Despite these good intentions and efforts, however, achievement and parent involvement remained low. Comer provided the structure and means to pull together all of the efforts for success under one umbrella. The Comer Process provided Oceanview with a mechanism for responding in a child-centered way to the changing needs of its students. A teacher who has been with the school for over 20 years reflected on how the Comer Process channeled a number of existing forces in the school into a more focused effort for change:

I think it is kind of interesting [how] the Comer Process [provided] labels or kind of crystallized attitudes that were already here at the school. I have been here for a very long time, probably longer than anyone else here, and the school has changed tremendously in that amount of time. The one common thread throughout those years has been the fact that there has always been a real concerted effort to have parent involvement and to communicate to the community and that became more and more of a challenge as our community changed from a white working class, middle class neighborhood to a very mixed multiethnic, multi-economic neighborhood, and now a lower middle class neighborhood. Through all of those years we have had administrators that have really cared about having parents involved. We had a PTA and then because none of them could really speak English, and we didn't have personnel to help facilitate that communication, it died on the vine. But during all of that time there was always a very honest effort to have parents involved either as volunteers, as room mothers or in the organization, the school site councils. It was this interest that was brewing probably over the last 10 years for having correct placements for students, meeting their needs educationally, making sure that the programs met the needs of the students, rather than plugging students into . . . classroom spots. . . . So the interest has always been there but the Comer Process in a way crystallized and helped to focus the process that was already here in that it gave a government principle for us to operate by and it helped parents feel welcomed. Teachers were always reaching out, but everybody did it differently and it was like some people were hit and miss and some people didn't do it as well as others and some people didn't do it at all. With Comer, it kind of made things uniform, it gave us a way of looking at our community and saying okay we can involve all of them and this is the way to do it.

Comer became a way for the school to frame goals and conceptualize the necessary changes for the school to "meet the needs of the school and community." For Oceanview, an important part of the Comer Process has been devising strategies to turn the school's tremendous diversity into an asset for meeting those needs. With the unique ethnic makeup of the school and community, the school staff believed that the best way to accomplish their goals was to respect and embrace the different cultures, using ethnic difference as a learning resource. As a teacher explained:

> One thing that we are really striving for as a Comer school is to try and bring the different cultures together because we do have different [language] programs. [The principal] was talking to us yesterday, saying that we don't want to have isolated cultures. So we do cultural celebrations where we learn about Chinese New Year, Cambodian New Year, or African History month. But I think what we want to go for is to have the children actually actively work with one another because they do have stereotypes. They come with stereotypes, and we want them at this age, in their formative years, to be able to work with other children and be free of biases and not just stay within their own community.

Multiculturalism and multilingualism, therefore, are not impediments to this school. On the contrary, they provide the opportunity for students and staff alike to learn about different cultures and to practice tolerance.

The Comer philosophy of decision making, which focused on the needs of children, helped Oceanview work through some potentially wrenching changes. The staff's reaction to a change in the school's schedule and attendance area provides an interesting example of how deeply the child-centered philosophy has permeated the school's culture. Because of the large numbers of students and lack of space, the school operated on a four-track system, which allowed only 75% of the students to attend school at any given time. The school had long exceeded its capacity, so the district decided to shorten the attendance zone from nine square blocks to six. This allowed Oceanview to change from the multitrack system to a single track, so that all of the students and staff could simultaneously attend school. The loss of three blocks, however, translated into the transfer of over 400 children and 20 teachers to other schools. These changes undoubtedly created a new set of tensions. The sharp decrease in numbers of students means that many of the new teachers would lose their teaching positions. The plan to downsize the school was made by the district office and some parents were upset that they had no voice in this decision. Surprisingly, most of the tension surrounding the reduction of the school's size was external, from parents and the community. Most of the teachers interpreted this change as one that was "in the best interest of the children," one that was consistent with the Comer ideology that drives all school-based decisions. Because they clearly saw how the reduction in overcrowding would benefit the students, most of the teachers exiting next year did not pose much opposition to the plan.

Building a bridge between the theory and practice of Comer enabled the school to smooth the various changes and transformations that it encountered. Staff acceptance and "buy in" of Comer as a governance structure, as well as a culture, is part of what makes Oceanview a successful Comer school.

SUCCESSES OF THE SCHOOL SINCE COMER IMPLEMENTATION

Since Oceanview adopted the Comer School Development Program (SDP), it has seen various successes, including increased parental involvement, improved school climate, and improvement in student achievement. Because Oceanview is a firm believer in the holistic philosophies of Comer, that it "takes a village" to raise and educate a child, one of the school's first priorities was to increase parental involvement and create a partnership with parents. Evidence of an increased parental presence is seen daily in the school. In the "parent room," there is a constant influx of parents from various ethnic groups mingling and working together on projects for the children to use later in the classroom. The presence of parents at the school is an effective and productive way for teachers to add more artistic and integrated lessons into the curriculum. Teachers know, for example, that if they need paper cutouts for a particular project, they can leave the materials in the parent room and the task will be completed. The parent room also serves a very important purpose by opening the communication lines between the school and parent community. To keep the parents updated on events and the details of the Comer Process, all major bulletins are translated into five languages and then posted.

Perhaps the biggest obstacle to parent involvement that Oceanview has overcome is the formation of the PTA. For the first time in many years, the school has an organized parent group. Previous efforts to organize a PTA failed as staff and parents were unable to get beyond language barriers so that they could unite around a common purpose. But, with the increased interaction among culturally diverse parents occurring in the parent room, and the critical role of the teaching assistants as facilitators and translators, language is no longer an insurmountable impediment. Rather, multiple languages and cultures are seen as a resource, something that enhances the multiple visions and voices in the PTA.

Another important initiative that boosted parental involvement is the district's Parent Institute for Quality Education (PIQE). Although not directly related to Comer, the PIQE addresses many of the needs the school focused on through the Comer Process. According to the district's Comer facilitator:

It [PIQE] was designed to teach Latino Spanish-speaking parents about the American school system, but that expanded to other languages. It was a six-week course, once a week for six weeks. You have all of the parents and then there were probably over a hundred kids to watch in childcare. I think hundreds of parents graduated from the program, so it is a big hoopla for these parents because many of them have never graduated from school. Everybody pitched in to make it special for them because that is the way that this school is. Everybody has to pitch in and I didn't hear any grumbling.

Oceanview's continued efforts to get parents involved have proven effective, as many parents now feel welcomed and are deepening their roles in the school. As one parent said:

I think that having the continual emphasis that your opinion is just as important has been very empowering. With a lot of new immigrant parents, it has helped them to interact. I felt really welcomed here to help with decision making and be more active. I know that my input and ideas are welcome here.

Since the school began to actively involve and include parents in all discussions, teachers and staff are now finding that parent impressions and attitudes toward the school are more positive, which in turn is changing the way the children feel about the school. Establishing connections and opening the communication between home and school cultures is one of the most positive aspects of the Comer Process at Oceanview. As Comer predicted, opening up such links has important educational benefits. Parents feel more comfortable, open up to the staff, ask questions, and volunteer information that may be helpful in assessing their child's' needs. The success of the strengthened partnership between school and parents benefits the children and adds to the inviting nature of the school climate. In such a climate, students are more open to learning.

The change in school climate to what was described by one teacher as a "high energy environment," is one of the many successes at Oceanview Elementary. Learning is exciting, and the children know they are in a safe and comfortable environment. One teacher said, "I think this school is like an island in the community where it can be a resource of safety and a place for students to feel safe. We try to keep it neat so that they feel comfortable here and they feel welcome here." The school, however, is not just a safe place for students. The climate of the school is such that the teachers and support staff also feel that they are working in a safe and supportive environment. One primary language teaching assistant commented that she particularly enjoyed working at Oceanview because she can help parents and students with her translation skills, but she also feels comfortable getting help, such as learning about the United States and American culture.

Teachers reported that the system of support and bonding that exists among the staff is largely due to the many changes the school has undergone in the past few years. For example, two years ago, a school calendar change allowed sufficient time for the teachers to attend staff development workshops and enabled the staff to work together on issues critical to the success of the school. Going through the Comer Process also helped Oceanview realize that everyone in the school had different expectations for children. This prompted them to identify the need to coordinate their efforts and work as a team to meet student needs. Thus, for the end of the year they decided to develop a unified vision of growth and achievement for students. Having the entire staff work together on a rubric provided the opportunity for group ownership, so that all teachers owned the criteria for teaching all of the students. Group ownership set the stage for what would turn into a supportive system of camaraderie. One teacher described the changes that took place among Oceanview's staff under the Comer model:

> I think that because there is more focus on supporting one another in supporting the students that the degree of cooperation has grown amongst everyone. We are more willing to look at change if it will help us to support the student and help the student to be more successful. We now are systematically doing placement testing for the second language students so that they are being placed in the appropriate classes when they first arrive, helping them to be successful when they first come in. I think that those are changes that came out of the more productive atmosphere. In a general way it trickles down to that so that everybody is willing to make changes and add the responsibility to what they are already doing if it is going to support the program and the children.

Ultimately, the cohesion among the staff, the improved school climate, and the increase in parental involvement all contributed to an environment that fostered increased student achievement. Oceanview's test scores have risen steadily since the school adopted the Comer Process. One of the major reasons for this increase is that with the structural changes made since the inception of the Comer Process, children are now placed in the appropriate classrooms and take the appropriate tests. Students receive educational experiences more tailored to their needs and are assessed more fairly. For three years, scores in every area on the Abbreviated Stanford Achievement Test (ASAT) showed steady gains, with notable increases in the scores on the Aprenda for Spanish bilingual students. The dedication of all stakeholders, as well as the placement of students into educationally appropriate classrooms, has made a tremendous difference in student achievement.

Principal Scythe emphasized that the many organizational and cultural changes that resulted from Oceanview's Comer Process have a common aim:

> All of the reasons for the teachers being well trained, our reason for looking at all of the issues and all of the developmental pathways and making sure

that each child is appropriate to be placed in the program, ultimately it is for student achievement. It took a long time for it to show, but then for three years we have seen improvement in student achievement, as well as all of the other indicators that you would look for like parents coming in and children being happy, children on task, parents and teachers communicating and staff members doing what they are doing. All of the things that really makes a school feel right. That is all happening. We have been showing it in our portfolios, we have been showing it in student records, we have been showing it in the reviews and suddenly the students standardized test scores came up too. I think that was the ultimate goal, to have the children and their families become more successful in the school experience.

For Oceanview, higher academic expectations for students, an improved relationship with parents and community, and a supportive staff and school climate were enough to prove that the school had achieved major successes in the three years it had been a Comer school. The increased test scores validated everyone's efforts by providing raw data to prove that what they knew was best for the children of their school was working.

PARALLEL INITIATIVES

Although Comer is Oceanview's overarching structural reform effort and guiding philosophy, the school also incorporated other new programs. Of particular importance here is that all of the additional programs and initiatives fall under the umbrella of the Comer governance structure, and are consistent with the philosophies and principles of the SDP. These additional components strengthened Oceanview's Comer implementation because the school community tailored them to the specific needs of their students and community.

One initiative that is in line with Comer, as it addresses both the cognitive and social developmental pathways and the need for community, parent, and school partnerships, is the FAST (Family and Schools Together) program. An intervention program that targets families with children from kindergarten to third grade, its purpose is to foster healthy academic and social development. It is yet another of the many efforts that the school has implemented to increase parental involvement and strengthen the partnership between the community and the school. Oceanview is one of 12 FAST sites across California funded by the Office of Child Abuse Prevention/Juvenile Crime Prevention. According to the district nurse, Oceanview's Comer-linked approach to the program is unique because

we are the only FAST program that is a collaboration with community organizations. Our commitment was in this community, to reach the hardest to reach families who were isolated either by language barriers, social barriers, any number of things. Our goal was to target those families and bring them into the school.

Oceanview's community-rooted approach to the FAST program reflects the Comer belief that family and community resources are essential to students' success.

One of the major instructional programs that Oceanview spent a year planning and will implement next year is Project More. The purpose of Project More is to identify the most successful strategies for helping second language students acquire the English language in a sheltered-content classroom. It calls for thematic classroom instruction; for example, using arts experiences to reinforce concepts in the curriculum, as well as cross-program integration. To support this integration, the school plans to have "literacy families," in which groups of children within a program work together to focus on language arts and reading. "Families" from the bilingual program and English programs will then be paired to work together so that literacy development within the bilingual programs is not isolated. The literacy families also include special education students and resource teachers, which will further bridge programs and unite the school's literacy focus. Oceanview's intensive and inclusive focus on literacy emerged from the Comer-driven analysis of student needs.

COMER AS STRUCTURE AND HOLISTIC VISION

For Oceanview, the link between school success and the Comer SDP is quite clear. Comer is not only a structural framework that governs the organization of the school but the ideology that allows diversity issues and other student needs to be addressed. SDP's child-centered philosophies permeate the school. The Comer philosophy undergirds the attitudes of the staff, drives change, propels team decisions, and steers classroom instruction.

Oceanview has heartily embraced the holistic vision of the SDP. In retrospect, staff said that they already viewed students holistically, but they did not know how to put that into practice. Comer provided that framework through the developmental pathways and the belief that collaborative partnerships with all major stakeholders contribute to a successful school environment. According to one teacher:

> The parents, the people that work in the community, the service agencies that serve our children, the staff and the children all have to work together. We felt like everyone had to increase their awareness together. Just having teachers wasn't good enough, just having children working hard in school wasn't going to be enough, just having the parents wasn't going to be enough. Everybody had to do it. So the Comer philosophy fit right into our

vision; it was almost like we were ready and ripe for hearing from someone how to put it together in a package. We had the feeling but we hadn't thought about "it takes a village to raise a child." We had always believed that that was the way. We also had for a long time looked at the various aspects of the child. We spent a lot of time looking at health issues. We spent a lot of time working on social issues.

In other words, working together collaboratively in a partnership between school and community is a long-held value that Oceanview has been able to put into practice using the Comer Process. Oceanview staff emphasized that for the SDP to work, active participation is required from all players to assure that all voices are heard and the children's needs are met in all dimensions. As one teaching assistant commented, " I think it is a great program because it is like running a government, where everybody counts; not only the main people, the principal, the administration, but the whole staff and the parents. I like it because you consider everyone."

Working through the Comer Process helped the Oceanview staff identify the need for more teaching assistants who spoke the languages of the students and families. These teaching assistants are integral to the working of the school today, as they are the primary connection between the school and the community. With 17 different languages and dialects spoken, the teaching assistants work diligently to translate all newsletters and notices to parents in five major languages and to provide translations at meetings and events. In addition to their traditional classroom assistance responsibilities within the academic program, teaching assistants also help teachers and resource specialists with speech screenings and other assessments of children.

As one teaching assistant described the newly defined role they play within the Oceanview community, "Since Comer I think that the emphasis is almost equally reaching out to parents as much as working with the students in the classroom." Another assistant said, "We help do screening for the speech pathologist for the students who are non-English speaking in all of the languages. I would say there is a more concerted effort for cooperation for all of the support to be able to help the students and also reach out to the parents." A teacher acknowledged:

> Yes the program has changed in the classroom so far as they are not primarily teaching curriculum. Now, they're responsible to help the teacher, to help the child know the regular curriculum, but we have changed the emphasis so that they're available for as much translations as are needed. Not only for written translations, for parent notices we send everything out here in five languages routinely.

The Comer Process also provided a formalized structural mechanism for all the major players to be involved in the school. In addition to all of the informal networks and collaboration among staff, the Comer Process created a formal governance structure for staff and community involvement through the workings of different teams and special interest workgroups. All of these teams operate according to the Comer guiding principles of collaboration, consensus, and no fault. Foremost among them is the School Planning and Management Team (SPMT), which at Oceanview includes the entire staff, as well as parents and community members. This arrangement is unlike other Comer schools. As one teacher explained, "We are unusual in that our SPMT is really our Oceanview Council and includes all staff. That is kind of above and beyond the Comer writings, but that helps us to have more buy in. It is not just representation, it is direct."

The Oceanview Council/SPMT is the school's large-scale planning, management, and evaluation team. It functions like a traditional town hall meeting, with as many as 50 staff, parents, and community members participating. A crucial part of the school culture already in place before the adoption of the Comer Process, the Council now operates by the Comer guiding principles. Oceanview felt that keeping this governance body open to all participants extended and deepened the principle of consensus, which is consistent with both the Comer philosophy and the school's traditions. A classroom teacher who is one of the co-leaders of the Oceanview Council said, "Comer has really taught us collaboration. We were already doing consensus with school site management, but there wasn't much collaboration. I think that no fault has made us kinder and gentler people." The main evidence of enhanced collaboration on the Council is the increased participation of parents.

It is important to the school that everyone's voice can be heard at these meetings. Everyone and anyone can attend meetings and voice their opinions and concerns, so that as a large group they can reach consensus and make decisions. Anyone who does not feel comfortable verbally voicing concerns may fill out an "item of concern" form. This simple mechanism allows a broader range of voices to be heard, as many bilingual parents do not feel comfortable speaking English in front of large groups. Significantly, it means that the strongest voices in the school and community do not drown out others. This forum keeps lines of communication constantly open and provides an important sense of responsiveness to emerging issues. Because there is no secrecy or exclusiveness as to what issues are handled and what decisions are made, everyone in the school and community feels ownership of the school.

Because the Council/SPMT is such a large governance body, issues are usually placed on the table and discussed there first, and then are referred to a special interest subcommittee. These smaller groups research the topic and bring the findings to the next council meeting for further discussion and, if consensus is reached at that point, a decision. It is important to emphasize that although Oceanview takes a divide-and-conquer approach to background work, all decisions are still made collectively. A teacher described how Comer's no fault principle makes these deliberations both more comfortable and more productive:

No one says, "you didn't try this or you didn't do this." It is more, "what can we do, what more can we do." . . . When you come to a team, they are not going to come to critique [your] teaching techniques or say, "You're not doing enough for this child." I'm coming in and they are going to help me so that we all together can do what is best for the student.

Using the Comer principles to achieve a child-centered agenda is a large part of what makes Oceanview Elementary a successful Comer school. A counselor described how the open communication and collaboration make Oceanview more purposeful and focused on student needs:

It is nice to have this collaboration so that we can bounce ideas and plans off each other so that we at least know that we are all going in the same direction. And sometimes our particular view point can be changed by a piece of information that someone else has gathered in one of the contacts that they have had either in working with the student or in talking with the parent. All of the sudden you see something you didn't see before. The collaboration, the working together, the reaching consensus on how is the best way of developing a plan for this particular student is paramount.

The Student Services Support Team (SSST) is another part of the Comer Process that Oceanview avidly adopted and used with great success. Although the Comer principle of collaboration is key to the success of all teams, it is especially critical for the SSST. This team has the difficult task of assessing and developing strategies to help children who are having problems in the classroom. The intervention begins when a classroom teacher observes a student struggling and contacts a resource specialist. The specialist then visits the classroom to observe and provide the teacher with alternative strategies and adjustments. The entire team, which consists of the classroom teacher, speech and hearing specialist, nurse, school psychologist, vice principal, and translator when necessary, then works through the student's needs together. The district counselor, who is also the SSST facilitator, explained the benefit of having a team approach to intervention:

Sometimes [teachers] come up and say that [students] are having a problem in the classroom academically because they are unable to focus, they are unable to sit still, or get their work accomplished. It is always helpful to have the . . . team meeting and have the parent there, so we all can say what we are seeing, not just what the teacher says. If we can have everyone come together to let the parents know what they are all seeing, about what they think should happen, the parents get a better idea.

Communication and collaboration between classroom teachers, resource specialists, and parents are key to adopting successful intervention strategies to help children. The team is very careful in making its assessments as members do not want to label children, especially if problems are related to health or language issues, which is largely the case with the immigrant population.

It is also helpful that all of the teams are interrelated and connected because they all report to the Oceanview Council, and staff participate on multiple teams. Teams are not just structurally related, but ideologically related. Whatever their mandate, all teams bring the concepts of the developmental pathways, the holistic vision of the school, and the principles of the Comer Process to bear on their work. One teacher said:

> Some people may have a special interest and may really be interested in developing the curriculum and the technology, but the focus is "how it is going to better the child?" Last year our curriculum team worked very hard in developing the language arts program in three different strands, so that we would be able to meet the needs of our bilingual students. We looked at outcomes of each grade level. That was applied and adapted by the classroom teachers. So all of that is interrelated, I mean, so all the other teams as well, the health and the human services. They are looking at how the services here can help impact and support the students. Support the families, support and classroom teacher, I mean, really all of it is interrelated. So there is a lot of collaboration, all the way around.

Furthermore, all of the teams are connected such that social service interventions and all other decisions are linked with classroom instruction.

The structure and theory of Comer provided Oceanview with a base and scaffolding on which to build a successful school. Principal Amanda Scythe is an important factor that keeps the scaffolding sturdy and in place at Oceanview. Ms. Scythe is a strong believer in the Comer ideology, and she uses its theories to keep the focus of the school on student learning and growth. Her modeling of the Comer principles of collaboration, consensus, and no fault through her own leadership style has guided the school toward success. According to district personnel,

> You have to have an administrator that believes in the model and models it where it works with co-workers and children. I feel that with Ms. Scythe, she models, she does walk the talk. There are some other principals that are at different stages of getting there and that is fine because Comer is the change process and we don't expect everyone to change their technique over night. I feel that Ms. Scythe was already a Comer principal before she came here. Because she works that way, I think it also touches the way that the other key players in the school are.

At Oceanview, the Comer Process is practiced from the top down and the bottom up. It is a culture that everyone, from administrators to teaching faculty to staff to parents and community, believes in and practices. It is the collaboration of everyone working within the same frame, with a common vision that has guided Oceanview in a positive direction. Here Comer is not just a program, a referential device or structure that can be placed on the wall and pointed to when needed. It is the culture, the vision, the ideology that drives all interactions and practices within the school.

THE INSTRUCTIONAL LINK: COMER IN THE CLASSROOM

Although the SDP provides an excellent governance structure and decision making philosophy, perhaps the most weakly defined link in the Comer Process is the connection between structure and pedagogy. The Comer Process sets up an organizational structure for schools but does not lay out specific instructional strategies for a school to implement. Oceanview, however, has filled this gap by using the Comer principles to refocus their instruction. Comer ideologies and developmental pathways permeate the school, most importantly at the level of each classroom. According to Ms. Scythe:

> One of the things Comer does is drive home that you need to make data-based decisions. [The process provides] no formal answers for curriculum other than what works. . . . So the difficulty is . . . finding what to measure [and] what the variables are and then turn[ing] them into effective programs. In that sense I think Comer does tie curriculum, because it doesn't give you curriculum but a process by which to look at what is working and what is not. A few years ago we were turning out kids who couldn't read at all, so we began using some very specific direct instruction strategies, not to the exclusion of the whole language piece but added it to the whole language piece. . . . The issue has been that students don't come with the skills to be successful in the programs as they exist, so we are continuing to modify the instruction practices to meet kids where they are.

Both the data-based decision process and the specific Comer principles led to changes in Oceanview's instructional philosophy. Using the developmental pathways as a pedagogical tool, teachers began to view children developmentally. Classroom environments are inviting, with multiple activity centers in different parts of the classroom. Activities are presented and changed at approximately 20-minute intervals, and lessons are integrated and interdisciplinary. This type of instruction is practiced in all classrooms—English, sheltered, and bilingual. Reflecting on the changes, one teacher said:

> I guess the one that stands out is the developmental pathways. They are always being used. We don't block students into just a mold that this is the

third grade curricula and this needs to be achieved. There is a willingness to look at why the child is not achieving. We look at all the background and all the issues that are impacting that child to meet a child at his level.

Part of Oceanview's accomplishments can be attributed to the school making a connection between the Comer Process and pedagogy. Data-based decisions result in classroom environments and instructional practices that are developmentally appropriate for children.

A VISION FOR THE FUTURE

Oceanview has a strong structural and ideological base, therefore its future with the Comer Process looks promising. The school understands that Comer is a process, not a program, and that they are constantly evolving. They attribute their success to the full implementation of Comer philosophies, but they also understand that, given their unique environment, they will never be able to rest on their laurels. Maintaining their child-centered focus will require Oceanview to constantly change and evolve along with the community. Their willingness to adapt to the changing student population and community sets them up to achieve their goal of meeting the needs of their children and staying student focused.

The intense focus on student learning and the numerous social support systems created in the school for students will probably keep student achievement moving in a positive direction. Spanish-speaking students are learning academic concepts and higher order thinking skills in their native language and in appropriate English Sheltered classrooms. In the past year, the numbers of English Language Learner (ELL) students who have transferred to English-speaking classrooms has doubled, thus achieving a goal set by the school's transitional bilingual program. With more students placed in correct classrooms, and with more receptive classroom environments, the number of students transitioning from the bilingual and sheltered classrooms should continue to rise. Keeping the pedagogical connection to Comer should continue to result in successful classroom environments and student achievement.

Perhaps the biggest success of Oceanview Elementary's Comer Process, an achievement for which there are no formal instruments of assessment, is the partnership and relationship the school has built with the community. With everyone working together for the common good of students, the school is bound for continued success. This collective purpose was summed up by the district's counselor:

My sense [of the school] is the inclusion, the receptivity to the families and their needs and being non-judgmental. The developmental view of the children where we take them the way they are. The open leadership, where everybody is a share taker. And I think too the original concept of James Comer that the community often centers around school is a very true statement. That is our collectiveness, that is where we can bring everybody together. We all focus on the comment of the love that we have of our children.

3

Gregory Elementary School

George W. Noblit
University of North Carolina at Chapel Hill

Michael E. Jennings
Tufts University

When you enter the foyer of Gregory Elementary School, you are faced with two sayings, two languages. In Chinese, there is a saying from Confucius engraved into a marble wall: "It is joyful to study and learn." In English, a scroll runs across the top of the same wall: "Education is the passport to the future and for tomorrow to the people who prepare for it today—Malcolm X." These sayings reveal much about Gregory School. They signal the two cultures of the school: Chinese and African American. They testify to the belief in education in each of these communities and thus signify a unity amidst difference. The two sayings also imply a more subtle unity that a casual visitor to the school might miss. Each of these statements is defiant. In China and the United States, both authors are officially regarded as subversives-authors whose works challenge the worth of the dominant order. Choosing a saying from Confucius is an assertion of people who have escaped Communism and who celebrate a different view of what it means to be Chinese. Choosing a saying from Malcolm X is an assertion of people who have been oppressed in a racist society but are proud of their race and its possibilities. Gregory School is the only institution in the community that brings the two cultures together. The children have even written a book of poetry about "them going through school together" with the title: "Making a Difference Together."

Gregory, a kindergarten through eighth grade school, serves a student body of approximately 650 that is half Chinese and half African American. The students are poor (95% are low income), and 30% have limited proficiency in English. The teachers are 48% African American, 26% Chinese, and 26% white. Located in Chinatown, its Chinese students and parents are mainly recent immigrants from southern mainland China. Many of these children do not speak English, and their parents often work long hours in Chinese restaurants to make ends meet. Just a few blocks away, but separated by a major expressway, Gregory's African American students and their families reside in housing projects that are plagued with gangs. Work is hard to find for these citizens of the United States, and welfare traps them in cycles of poverty.

Despite such challenges, the Gregory community is proud of its school. Gregory has overcome a history of racial divisiveness and united two communities behind the school. It has found ways for children to succeed in school, belying both beliefs about inner city, minority schools in general and its own history in particular. The Comer School Development Program (SDP) has been very helpful in these accomplishments, but the school had already begun its turnaround before it was introduced to the ideas of Dr. James Comer. In this school, the SDP built on a powerful base of support and an existing momentum of positive change: a dynamic new principal, a new focus on the needs of children, overcoming a shared ordeal that threatened to break up the school, and a new beginning in a new building. Although many of the pieces were in place before Gregory became a Comer school, staff and students alike acknowledge the value of the Comer Process in focusing and continuing the school's energy for change. As one third grade girl said when asked about the meaning of Comer: "Comer [means] a good school . . . [that] they have good people there."

This case study traces the many positive changes at Gregory School in recent years. Section II describes improvements in school climate, customs, and conceptions of children under the leadership of a new principal. These changes provided a crucial foundation for the successful implementation of the Comer School Development Program. Section III depicts how the school's newfound unity was tested and ultimately strengthened by a shared ordeal. Section IV shows how the SDP built on the school's developing strengths to focus the change process on student achievement. Section V presents a variety of indicators of school improvement at Gregory. Section VI offers concluding observations on Gregory's success with the Comer Process.

CHANGING CLIMATE, CUSTOMS AND CONCEPTIONS OF CHILDREN: FOUNDATIONS OF SCHOOL IMPROVEMENT AT GREGORY PRIOR TO COMER

In the late 1980s, Gregory was a school in trouble. While there certainly were schools with worse reputations in the city, Gregory had settled into a number of unfortunate patterns. Although the principal of some 22 years was highly regarded, in retrospect many people feel that he had succumbed to the beliefs and fears that the school's ethnic groups held about the other. These negative assumptions became institutionalized in the school's structure and divided its culture along ethnic lines. The Chinese were seen by African Americans as illiterate and foreign in both language and custom. The African Americans were seen by the Chinese as aggressive and unintelligent. The school accommodated these beliefs by separating the groups into different classrooms and, by default, accepting the stereotypes as real. The Chinese were ensconced in the bilingual program and stayed there even when their English language capabilities should have prompted assignment to regular classrooms. Thus, regular classrooms remained overwhelmingly African American. Furthermore, the school was accustomed to African American students being loud and disruptive in classrooms. They taunted Chinese students for their accents and demeanor and occasionally fought with them.

The teaching force was similarly divided. The regular classroom teachers (most of whom were African American) did not know what the bilingual teachers (most of whom were Chinese) were doing in their classrooms and vice versa. Each group of teachers saw themselves as protectors of their own students and distrusted the motivations and abilities of the "other" group of teachers. This segregation by program was replayed in the informal interactions of the students. As one staff member put it: "The Chinese and Black children didn't intermingle at all." Moreover, ethnic antagonism was being replayed in the community. The Chinese merchants in the neighborhood of the school did not want the African American children in their stores. Sensing that they were unwanted, the African American children deliberately "disrupted" stores. This escalated to the point where store owners began locking their doors when they saw the children coming up the street after school.

Although divided in so many ways, both groups in the school shared some depressing realities: low student achievement for both African Americans and Chinese, low parental involvement, and an aged building in severe disrepair. A former teacher summarized the state of the school and community at this time: "such a sad scene."

The veteran principal reached retirement age as the city schools began a dramatic reform process that gave control of the schools, including the power to hire and fire principals, to Local School Councils elected by parents. Gregory's newly elected Local School Council was majority Chinese, which gave the Chinese community the opportunity to hire a Chinese principal and effectively take control of the school. A variety of factors, however, caused the Chinese majority Council to reach across racial lines and offer the position to an African American candidate. This move was to have significant long-term repercussions for the unity of the once-divided school. A potential African American candidate, Assistant Principal Billings, told the Council that she was reluctant to move from her current position. Meanwhile, another African American candidate, Mrs. Knight, made the Council a bold political promise.

She told them that she was the only person with the wherewithal to get a much-needed new building for Gregory School. Mrs. Knight convinced the Council that she had the background in the district, a network within central administration, and the ability and knowledge to mount a successful political strategy. She was given the job and immediately began to work on both getting a new building and changing the customs of the school.

Mrs. Knight and Mrs. Billings, the Assistant Principal who had declined to be considered for the principalship, immediately began to work together to address fighting and disruption in the school and community. The restoration of a safe, orderly, and respectful climate was seen as a crucial first step on the road to school improvement. Agreeing that "We have to stop this fighting," they initiated a campaign to respond vigorously to student fighting by suspending students who were involved and requiring parent conferences to discuss the incidents. Less serious disruptions such as yelling and disrespect toward staff also led to parent conferences. In an effort to physically clean up the school, students writing graffiti on the walls were required to clean them.

Possibly as important as these initiatives was Mrs. Knight's leadership style. Her habit is to talk about issues publicly, immediately, and with as many members of the school community as possible. As Mrs. Knight says about herself: "I always talk about it!" With this level of public discussion, discipline and other critical issues could no longer be evaded as someone else's responsibility. Everything that happened in the school, whether positive or negative, was brought to the attention of everyone. Such public discourse motivated better discipline and created more open communication within the school than under the previous principal. It also provided public evidence that issues were being addressed and things were being accomplished. These measures began to alter the behavior of students within the school, but there were still problems between the African American students and the Chinese merchants. To Mrs. Knight and Mrs. Billings the goal had to be to "change the perception of the children" in the larger community, as well as within the school walls.

Mrs. Knight took to the streets after school with a dual purpose. The children learned she was a no-nonsense person within the school, but now they saw her walking up the street into the heart of Chinatown, overseeing their behavior there as well. This expansion of her authority into the community had dramatic effects on the students' behavior, as intended, but it also had an ancillary effect. "I became a visible factor in the community," Mrs. Knight observed, "and once they saw I was serious, the community began to press for continued changes."

The next step in changing the perception of the children was to let the Chinese community know that the African American students were "as smart as the Chinese" and to convince them that African American teachers could effectively teach their children. This was no small task and certainly not one Mrs. Knight could accomplish alone. She implored the Chinese teachers to act as intermediaries, "a voice to the community," to convince Chinese parents that moving their children out of the haven of the bilingual program and into regular classrooms was a positive change. Educators are highly respected in the Chinese community, and their words did indeed convince the parents of the merits of a regular classroom for their children.

As Gregory moved away from what essentially had been two schools under one roof and toward programmatic unity, there were costs as well. The Chinese community wanted after-school programs because the parents worked such long hours. They also wanted to keep a close eye on the school to make sure that their children were being served well by ending what amounted to ethnic segregation within the school. Thus, the Local School Council took on a more activist role and insisted on holding the principal strictly accountable for the safety and achievement of the students.

Mrs. Knight succeeded in satisfying the Council in no small part because of her focus on the children—all children—or "my children" as she puts it. She and the staff repeatedly refer to "the children" when discussing why something needs to be done, and parents have come to trust that this phrase includes the interests of all children equally. Invoking the interests of "the children" to justify decisions fits neatly with the Comer Process of child-centered planning but predates the introduction of the SDP at Gregory School. The pre-existence of this philosophy and decision-making approach at Gregory made the transition to Comer school status natural.

The dismantling of segregation dramatically changed the educational programs within the building. The bilingual program became a transitional program, and the regular classrooms took on the task of educating all students. Teacher assignments were changed to foster this integrated approach. Bilingual classrooms in the lower grades now have Chinese teachers and non-Chinese assistants. (Upper grades do not have teaching assistants.) White and Chinese teachers were hired so that the regular classrooms were no longer taught exclusively by African Americans. Significantly, these new teachers were not hired through the usual central office personnel process. The nontraditional approach to hiring provides important clues to the school's recent upward trajectory. Staff told stories about personnel being assigned to Gregory by the central office who were summarily sent back by Mrs. Knight when they proved to not fit the school. One story is of a maintenance officer who "borrowed" some electrical equipment, another is about a teacher who cursed at the children, and a third is about a teacher who left some students and grandparents at a zoo when they could not find the field trip bus. Much to the consternation of the central office, all were informed that they had no place at Gregory. Mrs. Knight refused to budge on these appointments and the central office eventually acquiesced.

Newly hired teachers were in some respect known to the school before a position opened up. Some did their student teaching at Gregory, some had families in the neighborhood, some attended the school as students, and some came directly to Mrs. Knight when they heard about the positive changes going on in the school and with the community. The dismantling of segregation within the educational programs thus provided the opportunity for the creation of a faculty highly loyal to the school, the community, and Mrs. Knight. In some cases, teachers commute long distances to be on the staff at Gregory. A special education teacher recounted that at the behest of her family she transferred to a school closer to her home, but within weeks called to ask for her position back. The working conditions at Gregory were so superior that her family came to accept her long commute and the longer days demanded at Gregory. For all the teachers we interviewed, long commutes (for some) and longer hours of work (for all) were seen as a worthwhile tradeoff for being at a school that is experiencing such success.

Throughout the early years of Mrs. Knight's principalship, Gregory was growing in unity among parents and community members, in the instructional program, and among the faculty. This unity was to prove a crucial resource for overcoming the rocky transition described in the next section and ultimately for successful implementation of the highly collaborative Comer Process.

BUILDING UNITY THROUGH OVERCOMING A SHARED ORDEAL

As Mrs. Knight tried to reduce ethnic divisiveness within the school and community, she simultaneously began the campaign to construct a new school. She faced many constraints. The local newspaper published a story arguing that there would not be enough money to keep up with minimum capital improvements in the district, let alone build new schools. There was also no available property in the area on which to build a new school building. Thus, it was likely that a new building would not serve the same community at all, but rather a subset of the existing community linked to a new attendance area. Parents and community members pressed Mrs. Knight in a public forum at the Chinese community: "How do we get a new school?" They not only expressed their concern about the existing facility, but their desire to see the revitalized school community stay together. In the end, she promised them a new school and sufficient funds to make it a school of which they could be proud.

At the time, there was only one Chinese member of the central school board. Mrs. Knight's strategy was to approach him with the support of the Chinese community and use him to gain access to the other board members. In turn, she assigned a parent to each board member. The parents went to the board members' offices, met with them, called them often, and even sat in the board members' waiting areas to insure that they and their school were not forgotten. In the end, the decision to build a new Gregory School was made outside of the normal capital budget deliberations. An uproar followed in which other neighborhoods and ethnic groups complained. Yet the decision stood, and Mrs. Knight proved her worth to the community.

In order to keep Gregory School in the neighborhood, the new building had to be built on the existing site, which required a move to temporary quarters. Mrs. Knight and the community were clear that the student body had to stay together and asked to be housed in an unused building. The central office, however, decided for administrative convenience that the students would be split up and sent to other schools. Mrs. Knight heard of this decision before it became public and once again rallied her community, this time at a night meeting at the school. A petition drive started, and in two days each central school board member received a packet of copies containing the signed petitions urging that the students be kept together. Simultaneously, a media campaign made sure that news releases were issued and local radio and television coverage was arranged. Clearly, it was a good story in the context of a city system that was undergoing reform to empower local schools, especially when the school played the story as "what are they trying to do to the children?" Indeed, Mrs. Knight was convinced that Gregory students did not have the necessary "survival skills" for the schools to which they were to be sent. The schools were quite distant from the community and reputed to be "gang and drug infested." As a result of this pressure, the central office invited Gregory School to select an unused building as an interim site. Ironically, Gregory was forced to select a building in a community not unlike those they had protested: distant and gang and drug infested. Yet, the school was kept together, an accomplishment not lost on the community, the teachers, and the students. This chain of events shows how adept Mrs. Knight was at employing the Comer strategy of "rallying the whole village," even before Gregory became a Comer school.

The trials of getting a new school and keeping the school together at an interim site were testimony to the power of Mrs. Knight and to the newly found capability of the Gregory community. Yet, it was the shared ordeal at the interim site that in many ways cemented the school's developing unity. Gregory's temporary home was in one of the most notorious ghettos in the city. It was too small, had no cafeteria, and required all the students to be bused. Yet, "it was the only place" where the school could be kept together. Gregory School insulated itself as well as possible. The students were bused across town together, escorted into the building by the staff, and not allowed out into the neighborhood. Teachers and classrooms were doubled up, two per room. Lunch was trucked to the site and eaten in the overcrowded classrooms.

These conditions would be enough to daunt even the most dedicated staff. The Gregory staff was just coming together under Mrs. Knight's leadership, and they were "scared." The threats of building a new Gregory in a different neighborhood and splitting the students as the new school was being built had been difficult obstacles. At the same time, there was all the uncertainty caused by the very recent ending of ethnic segregation within the school. Through it all, Mrs. Knight constantly reassured the staff that it would work, that they could survive this year, and that they would be in the new Gregory by the fall of the next school year. The teachers rallied and came together. As Mrs. Knight put it: "They had the commitment."

However, it was increasingly clear that the new building was not going to be finished for the next school year. This threatened to unravel all that the school and community had achieved. The teachers were getting "strung out" working under such difficult conditions, and the community was not pleased with the idea of their children being bused any longer. Mrs. Knight held a luncheon meeting with her staff, and after hearing their concerns asserted: "I'm telling you we're going to open these doors in September."

The building contractors finally admitted that the school would not be completed in time, but Mrs. Knight responded by informing the contractors that they should give priority to completing classrooms because her staff and over 600 students would begin instruction in the new building the first day of the school year. The contractors argued that this was not possible, but Mrs. Knight's response was unequivocal: "I told them they had to build around us."

The situation was inconvenient for teachers, students, and contractors alike, but as the year proceeded it became clear that Gregory School had come through a shared ordeal of considerable magnitude. They suffered but survived, were threatened but triumphed. What was once a divided school and community was now united with a new beginning in a spacious and well-appointed building. The accomplishments were legion: students were well-disciplined; the animosity between the Chinese and African Americans in the school and the community was put aside; ethnic segregation within the school ended; the staff united to the point that they insisted there were no longer factions among the faculty; they survived the move to the interim site; and a new school was built for them. Through all this, they even boasted that they "never lost one minute of instructional time." The accomplishments of Gregory during this difficult period and the newfound unity of the school and community put in place a firm foundation for the implementation of the Comer SDP.

FOCUSING THE CHANGE PROCESS ON STUDENT ACHIEVEMENT: IMPLEMENTATION OF THE COMER PROCESS

Gregory School had a full agenda during these years, making dramatic improvements in the school's climate and social environment and major changes in the instructional program. They were aware, however, that something had to be done about academic achievement. Ethnic segregation in the school's academic programs was over, but achievement was still low among all of the school's student populations. During the year at the interim site, the director of the Comer initiative for the city approached Mrs. Knight to discuss how the SDP could improve student achievement. By the time the staff and students entered the new building the school was using the Comer Process.

Given Comer's spotty history in the city, adopting the process was far from a sure bet for Gregory. The city's Comer initiative was not run by the central office of the schools but by an independent agency. Discredited by years of mismanagement, the central office was forced to agree to reforms that dramatically undercut its power, such as the formation of Local School Councils to govern the schools. Despite concerns expressed by Comer, the district's SDP initiative started by trying to improve achievement in some of its most difficult schools. But, according to a district Comer official, this proved to be "a mistake" for a number of reasons. First, these schools were in the worst situations in the district and unable to see beyond their immediate crises. Second, the schools were selected for the project and did not volunteer to be part of the SDP. There was, therefore, little of the faculty commitment so crucial to successful Comer implementation. Finally, the principals of the selected schools turned out to be largely traditional, "hierarchical" leaders. It was soon realized that both the selection process and leadership styles of these schools violated key aspects of Comer's framework, including the principles of collaboration and consensus in decision making.

After this disappointing start, the city's Comer initiative began looking for more promising candidate schools in which to implement the SDP. Gregory's high-profile political success in rallying the community to get a new building was attracting attention to the positive changes going on in the school. District Comer officials said they approached the school largely because of the principal's leadership style, one that "helps develop everyone in the building." According to them, Mrs. Knight was "conscious that she needs to pay attention to her teachers so they can pay attention to the children." Moreover, "the high expectations the principal has for the school [are] communicated all of the time." It was also true that when the Comer Process started at Gregory, parents were active supporters but were not involved in the daily life of the school. The district Comer director credited this to the ethnic beliefs of the Chinese and African American communities: "For the Asians, the school has all the answers; for the African Americans, the school was not welcoming them." Parent involvement was a recognized need that the SDP could address.

Although increasing parent involvement was an attractive feature of the Comer Process for Gregory, the central goal was improving academic achievement. Even though the community pulled together and the new building was completed, Mrs. Knight recognized that "we didn't have the test scores or the skills-even the Chinese couldn't take the test because they couldn't read it." The Chinese students could achieve in mathematics, but their reading and verbal skills held them back. Test scores of African American students remained stubbornly low. Moreover, the principal knew that even with all of Gregory's other achievements, "testing was serious business—it makes you or breaks you." The state was instituting a "high stakes" testing program and schools would be taken over if their scores were insufficient. Regardless of all the progress made, Gregory School still had to improve student achievement. To this end, the staff and community agreed to try the Comer Process.

The SDP trainers and school facilitators all emphasize that school development is a process and that is what leads to improved student outcomes. Yet, at Gregory School the process led to much more. According to staff members, the Comer training allowed the usually reticent Chinese teachers to "speak for the first time." The staff realized that even as they worked together for years and made many strides toward improving Gregory School, they never talked seriously with each other about their collective goals for the students and the school. Mrs. Knight quickly realized that talking changed the staff: "Now we had something to build upon." She said that over the subsequent years the Comer Process "brought out the Chinese teachers slowly." Indeed, today the Chinese teachers often share Mrs. Knight's public communication approach, even with newcomers to the school. Following the shared trials that brought the staff together, the Comer Process enables teachers to unite around the positive goal of focusing on the needs of children.

The Comer Process provides Gregory School with a number of specific mechanisms and organizational forums for bringing members of the school community together to identify and address issues of shared concern. One such mechanism is the Student Services and Support Team (SSST), a vital tool for focusing the resources of the school on the needs of individual students. The SSST, which meets at least twice a month, includes the assistant principal, guidance counselor, a psychologist, a social worker, the truant officer, a student intern, and parents and staff appropriate to the issues being addressed. The team often has a translator to work with Chinese families. The SSST is the mechanism for the school to discuss and work with students who are consistently having difficulty. Early intervention is a "hallmark" of the Gregory SSST. After the fifth week of school each year, teachers submit the names of students who they feel might benefit from early contact with the SSST. As one staff member points out, "we are dealing with all the social ills of the inner city struggle . . . violence, abuse, drugs."

For students with severe family issues, the SSST links with other community resources, such as the Chinese Service League, to help the whole family. Gregory School quickly realized, however, that existing services in the inner city are stretched all too thin, and therefore the school has tried to develop new resources. For families in dire straits, the truant officer, who is in touch with "the heartbeat and pulse of the community," assumed the role of obtaining clothes and food from charities and churches. This is, of course, important in its own right, but it also communicates to poor people that the school is there to help them. This directly affects the community beliefs about Gregory school, noted earlier by the Comer director, which had limited parent involvement in the past.

Additionally, the SSST wanted to get a graduate student intern to provide direct services (counseling, service brokering, family support, etc.) to students. The SSST successfully negotiated with the agency overseeing the SDP in the district to obtain funding for the position. While the existing guidance counselor is fully consumed with testing, special services, and academic guidance, the intern is able to work directly with children. As one staff member noted: "All the kids see him." The intern also plays a central role in dealing with the "global issues" affecting the school and students. For example, he decided that the students had little accurate information about how to promote their own health. As a result, he set up a "health day" for students to get needed information and learn about available resources. The SSST also works with the assistant principal on discipline cases, bringing another point of view and often an additional resource to discipline deliberations.

The existence of the SSST and its integration with so many aspects of school and community life has created a more supportive environment for students, teachers, and community members. The SSST allows teachers to be proud of the fact that "we try to take care of everyone." The SSST and its work directly contribute to the caring ambiance of the school. Moreover, the team is recognized across the district as unusually effective and is often asked to visit other schools to discuss and conduct interventions, assessments, and training.

The Parent Team is another feature of the Comer Process that has proven to be a valuable resource for the school. The Parent Teacher Organization (PTO) was supportive of the school and politically effective when called in moments of crisis. Yet, as noted earlier, parents were not involved in the everyday life of the school. There are good reasons for this. First, PTOs in general concentrate on supporting the school and trying to promote parent attendance at their meetings. In short, their goal is to generate a broad base of support, and PTOs acknowledge that this requires minimizing demands on parent time. Second, the parents of Gregory students have real obstacles to their active involvement in school life. The Chinese families work long hours and, although committed to their children's education, many simply are not available for a higher level of involvement. The African American parents live in housing projects that are part of gang territories, and walking from one building to another may require gang approval. Walking past several housing project buildings to get to the school can be extremely threatening, if not impossible, especially for evening meetings when gang activity is high.

The Parent Team allowed Gregory School to develop a small group of highly involved parents who are able to lead the more traditional PTO activities. To increase the integration of these parents into school life, the school employs many of the parents on the Parent Team as teaching assistants or as part of the after school programs. This provides needed income for these families and gives parents insider knowledge of the school that they bring to their deliberations. Other parents are recruited as volunteers and often work as unpaid teaching assistants in upper grade classrooms. This allows them to do meaningful work with the children and gain insider knowledge.

Members of the Parent Team meet at least monthly, receive training, are networked with Parent Teams from other Comer schools in the district, develop school events (including "Cross-Cultural Celebration Days" that emphasize the similar values across the two ethnic groups and a grandparents breakfast that highlights the centrality of grandparents in both cultures), and represent parents on the School Planning and Management Team (SPMT). The Parent Team enables parents to be an active presence within the school and helps the school to better respond to the needs and interests of the parents. This has resulted in a change in the ethnic beliefs that both the Chinese ("the school has all the answers") and African Americans ("the school was not welcoming") held about school. The district Comer director argued that through the SSDP, Gregory School "began to change those myths . . . more parents became involved—Asian and African American working together on racial tensions."

The SPMT is a third key component of the Comer Process that helped to channel Gregory's momentum of positive change. The SPMT is responsible for developing the School Improvement Plan. A large part of its work is responding to issues brought forward by the SSST, the Parent Team, the grade-level teams, and the principal. The SPMT meets monthly and operates effectively as a representative body in which each member is responsible for soliciting input from her or his constituency. It also serves as the liaison to the Local School Council, the school's highest authority, in the planning process. Since adoption of the Comer Process, the SPMT does most of the planning and then submits its work to the parent-elected Local School Council for approval. This allows for collaboration and achieving consensus, two of Comer's principles for decision making.

This past year the SPMT's major goals have been to increase student attendance, enhance parent involvement, and improve achievement test scores. The SPMT is considering an accelerated program and is working through issues of how to select students and teachers. They also are working on enlarging the after school program so that it may be open to all students, expanding the library and re-emphasizing the reference skills of students, and integrating bilingual students into the regular program. In addition, they continue to address cultural diversity and pursue grants, such as a proposal that funded hands-on mathematics materials for all classrooms. As the vice-principal noted, "we are constantly in search of additional revenues" to help teachers, and they have been very successful in getting grants.

Like the other teams, the SPMT reviews and practices the Comer principles of collaboration, consensus, and no fault at each meeting. SPMT members agreed that although they were doing a lot of what Comer expects before they were introduced to the process, Comer gave them "a name, a procedure." Moreover, many members of the SPMT commented on the importance of the no fault principle. This principle enables them to get past seeking who is to blame for a problem in order to focus on gaining consensus on what must be done. As one member described the process, "now someone has the job to take the concerns and do something about them." Teachers reported that the SPMT uses Comer's developmental pathways to diagnose what students need and address those needs in their local school plan. Yet, the school's pre-existing focus on "the children" means the specific pathways receive less attention than the overall orientation of child-centered planning.

The Comer Process also gives the staff and parents something else: "a direct path to voice concerns without repercussions." It is important to contextualize this statement. The issue here is not whether the administration is open to input. In fact, Mrs. Knight and the assistant principal have an "open door" policy that is used regularly. However, the principal is a dynamic leader and highly respected, and in some ways it is this respect that gets in the way of frank communication. People may be reluctant to bring concerns to the principal because it may be seen as an implied criticism of the administration. Having an established process for voicing concerns, guided by a principle of "no fault," overcomes this reticence. Parents and teachers are expected to state their concerns and participate in solving them. The SDP enables Mrs. Knight to be a dynamic leader without the threat of being seen as an oligarch. In fact, she argued that the Comer Process "tempered me" and concluded that "Comer made me an effective leader." In this case, leadership and involvement are effectively wedded.

"NOT ON PROBATION?": INDICATORS OF IMPROVEMENT AT GREGORY

The incredulous reaction of one former teacher to Gregory's achievements gives a telling measure of their progress. Having worked at the school before Mrs. Knight's tenure as principal, he fully expected the school to be one of the 109 city schools the state put on probation for inadequate achievement. He recounted the segregation of Chinese and African American students, the inadequate instruction, an uninvolved community, and the difficult and unresponsive students. Gregory School, however, is not on probation. Far from it. One district official described it as one of the "exemplary" schools in the district. In this era of high stakes testing, Gregory School is doing well. District-generated "school report cards" show that student achievement is increasing. When test scores for 1993 and 1996 are compared, this improvement is evident. A total of 13 tests were given to Gregory students, and 11 of them show dramatic gains, whereas the remaining two show scores holding steady. Scores in reading and math show steady improvement. Moreover, the staff and community believe they know why they are succeeding in a school that a few years ago would have predictably found itself on probation. Gregory declared itself a Comer School in 1993-94, and its test scores have been on an upward trend ever since. Staff and community members argue that this is no coincidence.

The SDP facilitated the focus on academics that was Mrs. Knight's primary goal once the school's fundamental climate problems were addressed. When the state reformed the school district, it prescribed a curriculum and designed a test that was aligned with that curriculum. Gregory School went even further. After the SPMT identified the need for a school-level curriculum alignment to get in sync with the new tests, a teacher led an examination of its entire instructional program. Teachers examined the textbooks and "aligned them across all grade levels." They also focused on "taking out things that were no longer necessary" to be taught with the state curriculum and testing program. Next, teacher lesson plans were aligned with the curriculum and testing. A computer program was purchased that provided teachers with an efficient way to generate lesson plans (and demonstrate their alignment with the curriculum and tests) that are turned into the principal each week. The district Comer director noted: "The instructional focus is coherent, aligned" and "coherency comes from planning together."

Gregory School is also taking advantage of professional development programs available through the district-wide Comer initiative; district programs on math, science and technology; and the local teacher academy. Moreover, the school tries to develop special instructional programs targeted to the needs and interests of its students, including a writing program taught by a professional writer, photography classes, and a program that encourages racial pride via African American newspapers. Despite these multiple forces at work, Mrs. Knight sees the Comer Process as responsible for the gains in student achievement: "There's something to be said about talking about children . . . working on the principles and a lot of meetings . . . but this is how to improve academics." The SDP facilitates what Gregory School wants and needs, and provides a central organizing force for a multifaceted approach to improving student achievement.

A staff member characterized what a student finds at Gregory School today: "Predictability, consistency, expectations, safety, and fun." When students were asked about what is important at Gregory, the most common response was "learning." For these students, learning is about "things to go to college," "so you can find a job," "to win contests," and "working together." These characterizations reflect both the long-term goals of education (college and working), the performances that demonstrate school and student excellence (contests), and a style of work that is highly touted by industry (working together). When asked what is their favorite subject in school, the students listed all the subjects, but also noted that their favorite thing about school is "working"— to get to "learn a lot" and "helping the teacher." They noted that adults at the school get excited when the students "do good in school and get good grades," "listen to your teacher so you know what to do," "always read the instructions before you work," "go back to the books and find your answers," and "be good and work in school." They also said their school is "the best." They summarized the changes at the school as "the kids have gotten smarter."

Staff members gave a long list of successes for the school. The Comer facilitator noted she "couldn't finish the newsletter because the new grants kept coming in." Teaching assistants commented on "the nice family atmosphere," much like a "small community," and said "we all try to get along." Teachers said "it's a comfortable place to be" and that the "children pull together in times of crises." Other teachers noted the "safe environment," "test scores," and "no fights." They said "we are the best" and that "our school sets an example . . . especially in a multiracial setting." Most importantly, the teachers "enjoy coming to work here." They believe that in the context of the larger reform of the city system "we're more on target here than any other school in the city."

The teachers also pointed with pride to the fact that the school is a recognized success in the community: "people are begging to have their kids come to school here." According to teachers, the community sees the school as having "a complete turnaround in a positive direction . . . not just average but above average." Teachers and community members agreed that "the school brings the community together." In part, according to a teacher, this is because at the school "we have the connections to defuse racial incidents." Even district officials acknowledged "everyone knows you here and will welcome you into the class." This is especially important because "there are gangs in both communities, so we have to work to dialogue." When asked about what happens to students when they leave Gregory, community members responded that "the values and [what] they've learned are the building blocks of their lives." Knowing what is possible at Gregory, however, has the community even more concerned about the high schools for their children. The desire to maintain the positive momentum of Gregory is so strong that the community, with the support of the school, applied for a charter high school for their children. They did not get their charter but have not given up. Their prior successes in educational politics leave them optimistic that they can succeed.

Even with this success, staff and parents noted that there are perennial issues that demand their attention. "Communication is always an issue," as is "parent involvement in a way that meets the needs of this community." Moreover, "many kids are dealing with violence in the community and abuse . . . also drug and alcohol abuse-across both races." Staff were pleased with the parent turnout at a recent arts-and-crafts workshop, but sober after being confronted with the many challenges the parents face in their lives: "The personal crises of the parents are daunting, but they feel support here and so they come." Staff noted that "teaching the two cultures to get along is our biggest problem," but then they listed a more traditional educators' list of concerns: "homework, discipline, school rules, relationships." Students recounted the persistent issues of their lives at Gregory: "arguing," "talking," "running," and "not working."

In short, Gregory School is aware of both its successes and its fragility. Aside from getting the new school, all the successes that Gregory has experienced require continued monitoring and development. The SDP is the mechanism they use to continue to improve. SPMT members credit the Comer Process for the school's "camaraderie," for the "excellent" discipline, for being "connected to other schools," and for the staff's "higher respect for parents." Moving forward, they say the school must use the process to address the continuing challenges of getting "more parents involved," having "counseling services expanded," and raising attendance and test scores.

CONCLUSION

Gregory School defies the stereotype of urban education. Gregory is an inner city school. Gregory serves poor people, people of color, and immigrants. It has a history of low achievement and ethnic divisions. Embracing the subversive spirits of Confucius and Malcolm X, Gregory School is testimony that education can be the vehicle to overcome the powers that define a person as unworthy. Regardless of its history and the stereotypes of wider society, Gregory School found a way to overcome racial divisiveness and be a good place for children. It also strives to become even more, focusing on raising the academic achievement of all of its children.

Gregory School has a unique history. Few schools experience the shared ordeals and accomplishments that this school has experienced. Clearly, much of what has been accomplished is due to the principal, Mrs. Knight, but she is reluctant to take too much credit. She said: "Let's just say it was the community" that makes all this possible. Certainly the community rose to the challenges her leadership issued. Whoever is responsible for the school's political achievements, they set in place a united staff and community who were able to see that Comer offered something for them. The SDP is their decision-making mechanism, a vehicle for continued instructional improvement, and a way to continue the successes achieved with the community. The SDP also balances the power of a dynamic principal and the power of an involved and committed faculty and community. Comer did not directly lead to any of the school's successes. Rather, it empowered people to make the decisions and act in ways that lead to better student achievement, parent involvement, community support, and faculty commitment. It is the people of Gregory School who are responsible for the successes they have achieved, but the SDP gave them a process that they use effectively to focus and continue their upward rise.

4

Merrit Elementary School

Sofia A. Villenas
University of Utah

Paula R. Groves
University of North Carolina at Chapel Hill

It is the first lunch period at Merrit Elementary. The song "La Marcarena" is blasting, and the kids in the cafeteria are laughing, shouting, and moving with the beat and rhythm of the loud dance music. The principal is late as he rushes into the cafeteria. He rolls up his sleeves, puts on a pair of plastic gloves, grabs a stack of trays, and runs down the lunch line dealing trays to the kids waiting patiently in line. Next he grabs a bucket of food and again runs down the line, scooping food onto each tray, quickly moving the line along. He walks around the cafeteria as the children eat, laughing and joking with them as the African American and Latino children move and dance in their seats to the beat of the music. After 10 to 15 minutes of mingling with the children, it is time for him to grab a new stack of trays, as the next lunch group is already beginning to file in. This routine will continue for almost two hours, as he must run the lunch period in shifts to make sure that all 1,275 students receive their free or reduced-price lunch.

Located in the urban flatlands, Merrit Elementary confronts many of the issues and problems plaguing economically depressed environments. Adjacent to the central point of drug dealing for the neighborhood, the school is nestled amid low-income housing and abandoned, dilapidated buildings. The community, however, was not always a neighborhood characterized by federally funded housing, inexpensive single-family dwellings, and low-rent apartments. Historically, the area was largely farmland, and until fairly recently the school served a predominantly Caucasian population. But with urbanization and "white flight" to the suburbs in the early 1980s, the demographics quickly shifted. The community around the school became economically depressed and predominantly African American. When the current principal entered the school, he faced the challenge of transforming a relatively low-achieving school covered with graffiti into a clean and orderly school that fosters academic excellence. The principal recounted:

> When I first arrived here I would have to say that the children, and the discipline had a lot to be desired. I remember my first introduction was an assembly with the students, they were getting up and walking out on me. I remember thinking to myself, am I that boring? And after a while I was wondering, where are these kids going? So finally I said "Just a moment. Where are you going?" The reply was "I have to use it." Well that meant they had to go to the bathroom, and mind you that teachers and everybody were in there and this was permitted, and so I said "no, this will have to stop." I really emphasized that the restroom facility should be used during recess time and that an assembly was equally important and it is classroom instructional time and that there would be no one getting up and walking without permission while people were up talking. This was also very rude, so I had to put into place some structure for the school. From there everything was uphill. My first year or two here I had teachers that I had to move out for hitting kids. I walked into a classroom to deliver the teacher her check only to see her with a belt wailing away on one of the students in the room, but what shocked me even more; after I walked in she didn't stop. I guess she felt, "well he seen me now so no point in stopping." I needn't tell you that I had to take action. So I had all of that going against me when I first came here.

Through his emphasis on order and respect, the principal was able to make major changes in school climate to make Merrit a safe, comfortable, and stable school environment. Today, Merrit is experiencing yet another demographic shift in its population. As Latino immigrants continue to move into the neighborhood, the community and school are becoming multicultural, changing from almost completely African American to almost one third Latino. This change has called for the addition of a bilingual program for English as a second language (ESL) students. The school now offers a transitional Spanish bilingual program for grades K-3, the goal of which is to use the native language for instruction until students acquire sufficient cognitive English language skills to function in an English-only classroom. The school now serves over 300 ESL students. The growing Latino population represents a new cultural challenge for Merrit Elementary, requiring the school to become truly multicultural.

The story of Merrit is also one of a process of responding to these challenges by creating a faculty that is united in its vision of high expectations and that provides role models for a diverse student population. This case study traces Merrit's use of the Comer Process to respond to these and other changes in a student-centered fashion. Section II recounts how a threat to the existence of the school built new and unexpected strengths. Section III discusses the inter-twined roles of strong leadership and the Comer Process in improving the school. Section IV presents evidence of the school's success. Section V shows how these successes are related to Comer implementation. Section VI describes the school's plans for moving the Comer Process forward. Section VII details some continuing tensions and challenges that underlie the school's success. Section VIII offers a concluding perspective on the past success and future prospects for Merrit's Comer implementation.

RESPONSE TO A CRISIS BUILDS NEW STRENGTHS

Merrit has overcome significant challenges before, even threats to its existence. With the discovery of lead contamination on the playground in the 1994-95 school year, the school was in danger of being shut down. Public health officials discovered that the park across the street from the school was a former battery factory and that the soil was saturated with high concentrations of lead and arsenic contaminants. In an effort to prevent the school's closure, the principal recommended opening the school doors to the local health department for a communication forum. Rallying the community in an effort to save the school, the principal led community meetings at which parents and the neighborhood could make their voices heard. The community made it clear to health officials that the school should be closed only as a last resort. After extensive testing of all students for lead poisoning, the only students who tested positive were recent Latino immigrants who apparently were exposed to lead from Latino pottery and traditional cookware rather than at the school.

This incident, which could have been so negative, was the beginning of a productive community partnership between Merrit Elementary School and the Department of Public Health. In the aftermath of the lead scare, the partnership resulted in monthly community meetings and opportunities for staff to attend special workshops on environmental issues. One public health official remarked that the lead issue was a turning point for the community because everyone came together in the effort to save the school. The principal used the newfound community unity and the recognition the school received to tap into more resources, including social and health services, as well as needed equipment and programs. Nurses and social workers were able to bring immunization vans to the school to provide immunizations not only for the children in school, but for all of the neighborhood children. The new partnership with the Department of Public Health proved beneficial for all stakeholders, as the community was able to receive needed health care and the department was able to obtain important demographic information that was traditionally difficult to gather because of a lack of response. With Dr. Price in the lead, the entire community responded and reaped the benefits of the school's new power. One of the greatest accomplishments of Merrit Elementary is that it is now the pride of the community and the center for community advocacy. The principal explained:

> Well when I think of this school as being one of the jewels in this community I see it as a model. This school is the center of the community, and it should be open for community activities. Yesterday the new city council member had to get my signature to use the school on a coming Saturday for a violence prevention [workshop] for the community. I feel we need to participate, we need to host whatever is going on in the community, so people get to know what Merrit is and what Merrit is all about.

Because Merrit is visible and recognized as an important player in the community, various people in the community have become involved with the school and developed attachments to it. For example, a local business owner donated computers to the school, claiming that he had special feelings for Merrit because of its outreach to the community.

As the school has been showered with community support and publicity, Dr. Price explained, "success breeds success. We've had a lot of positive press and this has resulted in contributions. All of this comes from exposure. I've never gone out to give press, newspapers seek us out." Indeed, newspaper articles were proudly displayed in a glass case in the hall entrance. Although many people worked behind the scenes to make the school the "jewel of the community," many attributed this success to Dr. Price's leadership qualities of caring and control.

"YOU HAVE TO HAVE A VISION"—LEADERSHIP, CONTINUITY, AND THE COMER PROCESS

Dr. Price is always visible at Merrit, leading and directing almost every aspect of school life up to and including the lunch room routine. He is a leader for both the school and community, and he sees the Comer Process as one that allows him to lead the school in the needed direction. Dr. Price said:

> What I appreciate about it [Comer] is it leaves it open to your creativity, you can take it as far as you want to go with it and as far as you are willing to work to put into it all of these creative ideas. I guess I could say I am a person who likes to generate ideas. I like to try them out. I like to see if they will work. To me that is Comer. . . . I think in my opinion you have to create a setting in which all of these pieces come together, your climate,

your intellect, your expectations, self-esteem of staff as well as the students, you have to put all of that into place for it to move just like a business. A business that sells and prospers is the one that pleases their customers.

As a school that runs like a small business, Merrit has focused primarily on the importance of order, discipline, and efficiency, as well as the unity of a family. Dr. Price said,

> Part of my philosophy is to push independence and show them to accept responsibility. I think about what Dr. Comer says—that there were thirteen children in his family and they all got advanced degrees. Somebody had to push them. Somebody had to believe in them for that to happen. That is our whole push here, is to expose our kids to the world outside of their community so that they can see that there are opportunities out there. Just coming back on the bus I heard the bus driver say, "all of the kids are so well behaved here." Your kids don't just get well behaved. You have to be like a parent with all of these kids. You have to really tie it in or connect it to their performance because it is a reflection on you. Another thing is we tell the kids how much better they are than other schools so that they really have the pride of achieving, performing, and winning.

For Merrit, much of the Comer Process is dependent on and works through the leadership of the principal. Reflecting the child-centered ideologies of Comer, Dr. Price plays soft jazz music in his office, has the character Pinocchio on the door, and has numerous trinkets that provide a warm and welcoming feeling to the children. He strives to make his office a place where kids feel comfortable. This child-centered ambiance, however, is evident primarily in the administrative areas, where the principal has directly sought to create an inviting environment. In places where the principal has little direct contact, such as classrooms, the environment reflects the dominant culture of the school, the culture of discipline and order.

The story of Merrit Elementary becoming a Comer School three years ago is one of choosing an initiative that fit well with what the school was already doing. As two of the administrators and a long-time teacher emphasized, they already had the child-centered philosophy, a leadership team, and the process of consensus and collaboration in place. Comer provided a new organizing focus for a change process already well underway. The school traditionally had a leadership team for shared decision making, as well as a child study team that functioned much like a mental health team. To help the school transition into Comer, the staff brainstormed about how they wished to restructure the school. Prior to the adoption of Comer, the staff decided that respect for opinions and voices was critical to the smooth functioning of staff meetings and that consensus was imperative. Although the school was proud of the success the staff had already achieved in turning around the school climate, they were attracted to Comer as a mechanism to improve academics (specifically test scores) through increased funds and the structured organization of decision making. Comer was also seen as a way in which they could advance a philosophy of education and decision making that they were already practicing—mainly child-centeredness, the belief in school and community partnership, and the process of dialogue in shared decision making. At Merrit, Comer is seen primarily as a philosophy of education emphasizing "family" relationships of caring throughout the school rather than as a mechanism for changing classroom pedagogical practices. One staff person commented on the goal derived from the Comer philosophy of the whole school working together as a team and family:

> I am not really involved in the classroom but what I have really noticed is that you have to work together as a team in the Comer Process and some people may have trouble doing that. Like she [fellow staff member] said, just being here just because it is a job. You have to really go beyond that if you are really into the Comer Process . . . it is kind of working together as a family and putting your self interest aside because we know the most important person is that whole family.

A teacher agreed that the Comer Process is about building a team:

> I think people that tend to say I'm going to do whatever I want to do . . . really don't understand Comer and the process. They might be good at what they are doing and I am not saying these are bad teachers and not efficient or ineffective teachers but it is just not understanding the total school picture.

SCHOOL SUCCESS

Administration, faculty, students, and community members claimed that Merrit Elementary was a "special" school that stood out among other schools in the district. Indicators of Merrit's success cited by faculty, parents, and students included good behavior, involvement with community, and high morale and self-esteem boosted by the many programs and activities initiated in the school.

Good Behavior

A major characteristic of the school that was stressed by almost all interviewees was that the children of Merrit are "better behaved" than the children in other schools. Good behavior and good discipline seemed to be a major defining characteristic of success at Merrit Elementary. The school adopted uniforms as a way to deter the use of gang colors, but also as a way to stress discipline. Staff and students alike commented that whenever they go out on field trips or attend competitions, everyone knows that the well-behaved students in uniform are the students of Merrit Elementary. One teacher said:

> Someone from the outside looking in would say our school is successful because all of the kids are in uniform and they are behaving well. I think it is because of the Comer philosophy and structure. It starts with the administration, staff teachers, and the formality trickles down to the kids. It makes for a better community.

Parents agreed that the discipline of the students is a major success for the school. One parent expressed the view that "discipline is phenomenal. This school is a family and although it is a very large family, it is very intimate. Students are always first."

Freedom of Pedagogy

The school seems to have adopted an agreement that pedagogy is the responsibility of teachers, giving teachers the freedom to implement their own teaching styles and strategies. Staff and administrators support almost any means of teaching, so long as the end result is learning and improved performance in students. They do, however, attempt to share information about the most effective practices. The principal remarked:

> If we go into a classroom and we recognize that something really great is happening then we ask that person if they would present that lesson to the staff in one of our staff development sessions. . . . I know we selected Mr. Green and Ms. Jones to demonstrate how they taught reading very effectively. Certainly these classes have really shown remarkable growth. In Ms. Jones' class, all of her children are reading in the first grade. She has a style that not many teachers can duplicate. Everybody is in a row and they are facing her and she goes over these words. You won't see a lot of fluffy stuff all around the room but her kids are reading.

A bilingual teacher agreed that the climate of the school and the directives of the principal allowed for freedom in instructional style and pedagogy. He commented:

> The school gives me the freedom to teach how I want, to use the materials I want to be successful with the children. I think all children should be reading in Kindergarten. You have to begin early with the kids and have high expectations.

High Morale and Increased Self-Esteem

Administrators, teachers, and parents noted the uplift in school morale since becoming a "successful" school, which for many teachers is directly linked to the adoption of the Comer Process. As one teacher said:

> I have not met a parent yet no matter how irate or upset that doesn't want their children to rise above. It is a real general, it is a good feeling here. Parents are willing to do whatever it takes. There are parents that are ill with many different kinds of illnesses but they all want what is best for their children.

Another teacher commented:

> I was surprised at the level of parent support. I guess I was going on the old stereotype, but there is a much higher level of parent support here, genuine support than in more affluent areas. Because here parents admittedly don't have any tools to work with but are willing to provide whatever they have.

Another result of the school's high morale, according to these teachers and to the principal, is the high enrollment. Many parents who move away from the area still insist on sending their children to Merrit Elementary. Administrators remarked that their "overflow" problem is a positive sign of the school's success because everyone wants their child to attend the school:

> The [overflow] problem is that the parents don't want to go to any other school and they will say we are just going to wait until you get an opening. We have people calling and calling and we don't have an opening. . . . You used to always have some vacancies, but we are getting more and more stable kids. Even if they transfer out they continue to come. The program has helped sell the school. That is why we have all those certificates and things out there in the hall.

A teacher agreed that the child-centeredness of Comer makes the school more appealing to the community and parents:

> I think that the message stands out that children are number one. It is the first priority. Most of the staff is committed to that. You care for children and you are willing to see them grow and become educated. I think that message stands out and that is why parents and everybody started getting in Merrit. Everybody is trying to get into Merrit.

The successes of the school are most evident, according to teachers and staff, in the morale and high self-esteem of the children. Much of this is expressed in the adult talk of "good behavior" and discipline, but it is also framed in terms of achievement and pride. Many of the children are involved in decision-making teams that came about as part of the Comer Process, whereas others are involved in various after school programs. A group of fourth grade girls talked about pride in themselves in terms of both their learning and their manners:

> In our class we have good manners when people come in, and hear our speaking, it is real nice. We speak appropriately and we learn a lot of big words like integrity and dignity and intelligence and attitude. That is pretty good because that's using your vocabulary a lot.

A teacher concurred in explaining the high morale and pride of her students who are enthusiastic about learning. She said,

> I perceive it as successful when my students want to come to school. They don't want to stay home, they want to be here. When the bell rings they are not looking like, "gee let's get out of here." They move through activity to activity with joy and expectation and I think that helps me view the school as successful when I see kids wanting to be here.

High morale for students has translated into high teacher enthusiasm. One teacher said, "I love what I do. I like the children. I like seeing them find successes when they think they don't have any and they do. That is just the most worthwhile thing getting up every morning to do because it is just a joy."

Activities and Programs

According to parents and to the children in particular, it is the many activities and programs that make this school special. For example, the school has an oratory group that was asked to perform at the mayor's educational summit last year and a student council that was responsible for building civic responsibility in children by conducting elections and setting up voting booths. There is a Student Site Planning Management Team that started under the Comer Process and involves all student leaders and officers of school clubs. The Safety Patrol takes on safety issues and was responsible for getting signatures on a petition for speed bumps on the main street of the school entrance. The students are also involved in MESA, an after school program with the purpose of getting children excited about math and science. One teacher commented,

One thing that I hope is that children can be successful and find that success because there are so many [opportunities] here of bringing that out. It is not just limited to a particular area or particular activity. There are so many things that are going on that every child should be able to experience some success.

SCHOOL SUCCESS AND THE CONNECTION TO COMER

The story of Merrit Elementary's recent successes blends the effectiveness of Dr. Price and the Comer School Development Process. In the accounts of students, parents, and staff, the principal's leadership and the Comer Process are fully intertwined. In fact, it seems that Comer has become the vehicle by which Dr. Price exercises his leadership and authority to secure the climate and the creative use of resources he feels are necessary for the academic and social success of Merrit's students. Nothing happens in the school without Dr. Price directing it—everything from the lunch routine, to the new Bilingual Advisory Committee meetings, to the Student Site Planning Management Team, to the fifth grade graduation. Given this level of direction from the top, the Comer Process is a crucial mechanism for balancing the principal's leadership with extensive participation.

Yet, it is also acknowledged that it is Dr. Price's leadership and encouragement that keeps the staff on track. As one very involved teacher commented, "a lot of it [the success of Comer] is because of Dr. Price. He keeps us on task. I think a lot of people would slough off if he wasn't involved in it totally." Another teacher commented on the positive trend she saw in the decentering of authority and the role of Comer in this process. She explained:

Well, pre-Comer we were on committees and what not but I feel that as we are getting more into Comer there is more collaboration, there is more trying to reach consensus on things. We all come with our own basic ideas, needs and wants. I think that as teachers try to work together and staffs and communities try to work together it is not always easy at our school because everybody is involved in so many things that I think we have trouble sometimes meeting challenges that are there in front of us but we try. I think trying to involve more people in decision making, using those stakeholders and things like that. Whereas before it was just, "do this." Now I find that the administration does try and involve more teacher input into things and getting us to be more involved in what goes on and that is not always an easy task. I think we have made strides in the right direction, hopefully.

In exercising his leadership, Dr. Price has embraced wholeheartedly the philosophy of child-centeredness. He commented,

> If you stick to what is best for the children, you don't get stuck in battles of "why do we do this." People don't understand how we can have a School Planning and Management Team and not have big disagreements. It's because all decisions are made for the kids.

Certainly, on the Comer teams, there are so many different staff represented that shared decision making becomes vital. Dr. Price very much delights in the ways in which staff and parents come to make decisions, and he takes pride in the collaboration and collectiveness that is involved. He explained:

> What is good about a Comer school is that on your site planning management team, everybody in the school is represented . . . to me that is where Comer fits in because in our site planning management team we have everybody represented and so your classified workers are quick to speak up and say well the teachers can't speak for us because we have rights too. I think that that is a very good point, it is a very valid point. We have made extra effort to include classified [employees] as equal partners in our school and that is something I have always worked for. They have just as much voice as anyone else because they are all touching the lives of children. Our site planning management team teachers' representatives are elected and the first group was appointed because we wanted people who were really interested and were creative and who had some ideas to offer and not to just be there to stop the progress or to rub shoulders with the people in charge so that you can seem important. That wasn't what our site management team was about, it was to be a working team for change.

Another administrator echoed Dr. Price's words:

> I see it [Comer] as bringing the school together, setting the stage. It's like the pulse of the school. It's the main thing that I see it's doing. We're doing good, we've got our problems but we work well together, the Comer Process along with the three of us [administrators]. . . . Comer is about involving students, staff, parents and community in decision making and everything related to students. We can't do it alone and that's what Comer teaches us. I really love the Comer Process.

One of the most successful manifestations of the Comer Process at Merrit is the Student Site Planning Management Team (SSPMT). It is made up of all the students who ran for student council and representatives from all student groups. For Dr. Price, this is the most powerful group and his personal pride. He explained that "they [the students] openly tell you what they need." In this way, students feel empowered to have a voice in the school and to make things happen.

"COMERIZING" SUCCESSES FOR THE FUTURE

Although the teams seem to be working in a "Comerized" fashion, employing the guiding principles of collaboration, consensus, and no fault, the challenge for Dr. Price is to make the SDP pervasive throughout the school and embraced by all the teachers. To this end, Dr. Price targets Comer resources toward new teachers in order for them to learn about the process as soon as they come to Merrit. One new teacher comments on this point:

> There is tremendous support here for new teachers being a part of the Comer Process. We go to workshops and come back to implement what we have learned. We also have mentor teachers on site. I think the reason the school runs smoothly is because everything is child oriented.

Evaluation of how the teams work is also "Comerized" in that there is a process of collective reflection involved. Dr. Price explained:

> Part of our philosophy too is that we have more reflections and reflection is feedback in a non-evaluative sense, coming from the classroom teachers, coming from the committees, all of the major committees I am asking for reflections on. The Child Study team or the Mental Health, the Language Assessment team, the SARC which handles discipline problems. I am asking them to give me a year-end reflections report that is in this weeks' bulletin. I want to know how many cases did you see, cases do you have that you re-evaluated, how many do you have pending that must be carried over and what were the trends that you saw in all of this?

The Comer Process is also carried over into the school's curriculum alignment plan that is currently in development. The school, led by Dr. Price, is putting together its own curriculum alignment plan beginning with grades 1-3 in reading and language arts. The idea is to develop these grades and subjects first and then move to a plan for the other grades and for all the subject areas of study. The plan conforms to district standards but also to the Comer developmental pathways. Dr. Price explained that not only is the plan user-friendly and includes chapters and tests, but it clearly delineates the ways in which the curriculum and suggested activities meet the Comer developmental pathways. The Kinder Store activity, for example, as explained in the plan, meets 3 of the 6 pathways—cognitive, social, and speech and language.

In addition to the teamwork philosophy and the child-first perspective, Comer is seen by many at Merrit as being tied to the influx of new programs and technology. Indeed, money from being a Comer demonstration school has helped to purchase a lot of equipment and to make links to university programs. However, it is Dr. Price's ingenuity in making the school available to the community and bringing publicity to the school that has given the school access to many new resources. In this sense, the success of programs and the role of the school in the community is not a product of the Comer Process but of the efforts of Dr. Price and his supportive administrators. Being a Comer School provides the extra push, resources, and publicity that Dr. Price needs to carry out his vision for the school. Comer came into place at the right time because it also provided a structure by which to govern the school, involve others, and balance the principal's strong leadership with increased participation from parents, teachers, and students.

It is difficult to determine how much of the success of the school is due to the Comer Process and how much to strong leadership. But, as Dr. Price has so often emphasized, Comer is a process, not a program, and not a prescription. Caring and control are common descriptions of a powerful leader whose changes have contributed to a better climate, increased resources, student empowerment in decision making, and more recognition for the school. Because Dr. Price is into everything at all times, he is often stretched to the limit when it comes to responding to ideas and concrete actions that other teachers and staff might contribute. Indeed, the best prospects for Merrit's future lie in the redistribution of responsibility and authority among all teachers and staff. The Comer Process is starting to take the school in this direction. This is in fact Dr. Price's greatest wish—the creation of a broad base of support for the continued excellence and improvement of the school via the Comer Process. He explained his suggestions for the Comer Process in precisely this area:

> [The Comer people should] Provide more opportunities for other stakeholders in the school to come together with other Comer schools so that it is not a principal's academy. You also need the secretary who is very important. She needs to be able to go back to Yale and meet and study and have the Comer School Development Process shared and for the secretary and clerical workers to give input. I think you need the custodian. He needs to get that opportunity and certainly the teachers need to have that opportunity. I feel that it is not enough to have a principal's institute and then the principal comes back and tells everybody how to do it. You need to involve them. The reason that I know that it works, we had a slight taste of it where we took myself, two support teachers, and two parents back east for the institute. I mean, just seeing those parents go back and take a picture with Dr. Comer. We haven't even had a chance to develop it. Then for them to be able to sit in a room and participate in a discussion about Comer, hear from other schools and then realize that we are not so bad off after all. We are doing some good things. I think that is what should happen. I would like to see that happen. I would like to see that whole circle widen so that you are not just working with your district liaison people, the university people, and the principals. The program can't survive unless you have that broad-based support.

Creating a broad base of support would also mean making more concrete the fledgling efforts to involve linguistically diverse families, such as the Latino community, in the Comer Process. The processes of consensus, collaboration, and no fault must be experienced by teachers, staff, and parents on their own terms. Child-centered planning and the use of the developmental pathways would also press teachers to consider what pedagogical strategies are developmentally appropriate for the children, putting order in its appropriate place. What Dr. Price must not lose is his creative vision of where the school should be headed. Dr. Price's words eloquently speak to this vision:

> Well, the concluding remark would be that I am a firm believer in the Comer Process. I like it because it isn't a rigid formula that you must follow or document, dogma. I think that you have to be creative for it to be successful, you have to have some vision of where you want to go, what you want for your school community; because if you don't, if you are looking for something to latch onto, you will be lost. I believe that is the way it should be.

The future of Merrit shows much promise as the school continues with more projects and programs and acquisition of new resources and technology. Dr. Price explained the plans for the future:

> Every main building will have Internet and Internet access and cable access. I feel very good about both because the cable access will involve what they call distance learning. We are taking Spanish as a foreign language so all of fourth and fifth grades will be able to get Spanish as another language here through this. It is live, it comes out of Los Angeles. We do distance science now, but we are really going to push the foreign language in. The literature is going to be a focus. Right now I am finishing up the literacy plan that we have and it is going to be tied into reading so that we read aloud in all the classrooms, guided reading, independent reading, shared reading. Then the writing, shared writing, independent writing but our staff development will focus on all of the subareas I guess you could say of reading and written language.

TENSIONS AND CONTINUING CHALLENGES

The future of Merrit Elementary will be shaped by some tensions that underlie the school's successes. One major challenge is fostering full participation in the Comer Process on the part of the school's growing Latino community. Currently, Latino teaching assistants and parents are too often outsiders in the Comer Process and in school culture generally. A major clue to this is that Latinos do not seem to share many of the perspectives on the school's success offered by other school participants.

Merrit is making efforts to get the Latino Community more involved in the school. In an effort to accommodate the needs of the large Spanish-speaking population, the school holds Bilingual Advisory Council meetings for Latino parents to voice their concerns. In these meetings, the principal tries to make the parents feel comfortable and asks for their involvement in district meetings, assuring them that transportation and child care will be provided by the school. Despite his offers, no parent willingly volunteered, with most saying that they wouldn't understand the meetings. The school's bilingual coordinator, who attends the School Site Planning and Management Team meetings as part of the Language Assessment Team, looks at issues of language for poorly performing students. Merrit holds the largest bilingual parent meetings in the district. Yet, as the bilingual coordinator commented, she wishes there was more parent participation in the school and on the SSPMT. Latino parents overwhelmingly did not know what Comer was and few were aware of the meetings. A few said they had stopped going because there were not very good translators at the meetings and they did not know what was going on. Others said they had not heard of these meetings or were not invited to them.

Thus, despite the efforts of Dr. Price to listen to these parents' concerns and the efforts on the part of another administrator, who is a native Spanish speaker, the involvement of Latino parents remains a major challenge for the school. There were indeed many staff members Latino parents could go to for help, but these connections were not being made. In addition to being less involved in the school generally, some Latinos had a very different perspective on the school's climate. For example, many Latino parents and staff did not view discipline at Merrit elementary as an element of success in the school. They, in fact, commented sharply on the lack of good behavior and discipline and referenced their home countries and cultures as the standard. One staff person who had children in the school commented in Spanish: "At school there are many discipline problems, in general the children aren't how I'd like them to be, with whom I'd want my children to go to school. I'd like them to be more respectful to the adults [translation]." She went on to say that there are some teachers who do teach children to be respectful but "there are a lot of other classrooms in which there isn't respect."

Spanish-speaking parents also disapproved of other children's behavior. They felt that their own children became the targets for the "bad" behavior of the English-speaking children, whether they be African American or assimilated Latino. Parents told stories of their children being taunted by other children who they deemed aggressive and disrespectful. In doing so, they alluded to tensions in race relations between themselves and African American families. One parent commented, "It's like they [African American children] have a lot of anger towards them, the Latinos and more so if one's quiet like my [daughter]."

It is important to recognize here that the meaning of "good behavior" and "good education" is culturally specific. Latino parents' definition of education encompasses the whole social and moral education of the child. As has been documented elsewhere (see Valdes, 1996; Villenas, 1996), Latino parents, and Latina mothers in particular, claim the higher moral ground in the education of their children in comparison to their views of the way children are educated in the United States. For this reason, whereas good behavior and discipline are deemed a success by most at Merrit Elementary, Latino parents perceive the socialization of children as inadequate in the United States, with Merrit but a case in point.

A second tension involves a sense that the school has an "in-group" of faculty who are strongly involved in Comer decision making and an "out-group" who remain uninvolved. Although the high morale and enthusiasm of many teachers high was tied to their perception of Merrit Elementary as a "special" school, there were some who did not share the high morale. These teachers were isolated and largely stayed within the confines of their classrooms. As one of the in-group teachers noted, people had been reelected repeatedly to the Comer teams, excluding others from participation. Out-group teachers maintained their enthusiasm with respect to their own students, but they did not see themselves as part of a team who worked together to make this "special" school happen. This in-group-out-group tension was exacerbated by staff turnover. As one teacher explained:

> We have a lot of turnover every year. Especially with smaller class sizes and people move around the district. Basically I think that the people that are truly committed have been here for five years or more and intend to stay. Like I said, I have been here for many years so I think that I intend to stay. . . . But if you had someone come in who wants to make changes it wouldn't work.

However, staff turnover is precisely what Dr. Price needed in order to reconstitute faculty unity and regenerate Comer. Indeed, as Dr. Price and supporters of Comer noted, the biggest barrier against the implementation of Comer and the processes of collaboration, consensus, and no fault has been the bifurcated faculty. Tensions and divisions among faculty into an in-group and out-group were based on white-black racial lines, particularly with respect to veteran white teachers who were teaching before the school experienced an all African American administration. Dr. Price talked about some teachers' racism and lowered expectations for African American children. These problems have long been part of the school's history, but according to the administrators, it is a lot better today than it was some years ago, particularly as more African-American and Latino teachers have been hired.

In order for the Comer Process to move forward, Dr. Price explained that faculty unity had to be in place. This year, teachers who were not responsive to students or who held deficit views of the diverse student population were helped to leave. Over one quarter of the faculty received offers for new and better positions. They were replaced by new "role model" teachers who were then trained by the administration and lead teachers on the Comer philosophy. The reconstitution of faculty unity not only regenerated Comer but became a basis for solving instructional problems.

The third tension in Merrit's Comer implementation is between philosophy and practice. We observed that there was a wide range of instructional strategies and pedagogies. Although Dr. Price has the policy of allowing teachers pedagogical freedom, it seems that the school's child-centered philosophy is not translated to instruction that allows all children to learn, particularly English-language learners not in bilingual classrooms. Many classrooms are arranged in rows of desks rather than in centers of activities that might allow more opportunities for students of differing abilities and languages to grasp the concepts taught. There is ability grouping in the classrooms rather than heterogeneous grouping, even in bilingual classrooms. There are very few signs of integrated curriculum. Rather, all the subjects are neatly divided. Indeed, the way in which Comer is translated into effective instruction at Merrit is in terms of effective discipline and competition with other schools. "But they are reading," is the comment that was often heard to justify the emphasis on order. Effective discipline and school competitions hide the tension between the Comer philosophy and teaching practice. Yet, with the rejuvenation of the faculty, the administration is at the same time focusing on curriculum alignment and child-centered innovation in teaching practices.

CONCLUSION

Merrit Elementary School has had many successes in what is an otherwise depressing environment. The community has come to appreciate the school's efforts and see it as a source of pride. As one teacher put it: "No matter what else they do, they are in support of the school." Dr. Price and the Comer SDP together have made much of this possible. Yet, in spite of the SDP and Dr. Price, challenges remain. The school is struggling with becoming truly multicultural. Creating faculty unity and expanding the base of participation in the SDP, as Dr. Price wishes, will be necessary to reduce in-group/out-group tensions among staff and between African Americans and Latino parents and staff. Finally, the SDP potentially has its most difficult challenge in fully translating Comer's philosophy into teaching practice because this issue intersects with the other two tensions and because enforcing a particular pedagogical approach is often divisive in schools. However, the school stands to gain with the integration of new faculty who come with new pedagogical ideas, who honor and respect diversity, and who are excited about their participation in the SDP. Merrit School has rallied to address great challenges before and has the promise to resolve these as well.

5

Trivette Middle School

William W. Malloy
Joseph M. Rayle
University of North Carolina at Chapel Hill

The day begins at Trivette Middle School with the arrival of the school buses and parents dropping children off. An assistant principal and other staff members oversee the orderly unloading and procession to homeroom classes, which at Trivette are called "Advisor-Advisee," or AA. As the students come through the front doors, there are signs welcoming parents, a banner that declares Trivette to be a Comer School, and posters that outline the developmental pathways and guiding principles of the Comer Process. In AA, some students receive academic tutoring. After school, some students meet with "buddies" who are mentors for a variety of issues, including self-esteem, homework, and reading. These "buddies" are provided by a local manufacturer that has taken an interest in the school. In addition to the "buddies," it also provides school supplies at the beginning of the year and prizes for successful students who are recognized at honors assemblies.

However, the Comer SDP at Trivette is far more than banners and posters. Throughout the day, tangible signs are evident of the positive changes happening in the school. Class changes are orderly. At lunch, it is not uncommon to see African American and white students eating and socializing together. Students clean up after themselves, even wiping off tables after eating or mopping up a spill. In the course of the day, the staff members in charge of student discipline are guided by the SDP principles of consensus, collaboration, and no fault, as well as the developmental pathways. By thinking through the developmental pathways staff try to pinpoint the exact cause of a student's behavior (e.g., physical, social, or ethical) rather than just focusing on controlling the immediate manifestation of the problem. Although some discipline problems persist, there are fewer of them since the school adopted Comer. In staff meetings, the principal frequently refers to the three guiding principles and the developmental pathways, urging teachers and members of the various school teams to take them into account when making decisions.

This orderly, positive, and focused environment is a far cry from the Trivette of a few years ago. This case study describes Trivette's turnaround and the role of the Comer Process in enabling positive change. Section II portrays the difficult conditions at Trivette prior to Comer implementation, with a particular focus on the void in leadership. Section III describes how a new principal was able to fill that void and use the Comer Process to tap the school's hidden strengths, enabling it to embrace challenges successfully. Section IV presents specific indicators of Trivette's success with Comer in four areas: school climate, instruction and student achievement, parent involvement, and partnerships with the community. Section V discusses the continuing challenges the school faces. Section VI analyzes the factors supporting the sustainability of the Comer SDP at Trivette. This section makes it clear that although the leadership of the current principal was vital in initiating the Comer Process at Trivette, there are now a number of structural and cultural factors beyond leadership that will support continued success. Section VII offers concluding observations on Trivette's Comer implementation.

A SCHOOL ADRIFT

Trivette is a medium-size middle school serving a majority African American population in a southern factory town. The school was created in the late 1960s during the integration of the school system. At the time of its creation, the population was predominantly white. Trivette Middle School was originally part of the city school district until several districts were merged in 1993 to form a countywide school district. The school is located in a community that reflects an interesting mix of race and socioeconomic levels. If one maps the school attendance area into a series of concentric rings with the school in the middle, a pattern of race, occupations, and housing emerges. In the inner ring, the school is immediately surrounded by residences that are in the upper end of the moderate price range. These homes are occupied by predominately white wage earners in professional- to skilled laborer-level jobs. Many of these wage earners do not earn a living within the community's boundaries. In the next ring, the homes are modest single family dwellings. The wage earners in these neighborhoods, who represent a combination of majority and minority ethnic backgrounds, are semiskilled to skilled laborers who earn a living within the community's industrial complex and service industry. The outer ring of the circle is composed of low-income single-family housing interspersed with public housing projects. The individuals in these neighborhoods are either welfare recipients or unskilled laborers.

Prior and subsequent to the merger, Trivette did not always enjoy a favorable reputation. From 1990-95 in particular, the school was known as a place where education was mediocre, the staff were indifferent, the administration was nonsupportive and transitory, parent participation was low, and the atmosphere ranged from disruptive to unsafe. Whenever possible, residents of the community sent their children to other schools in order to avoid Trivette. It was widely seen as an unsafe school. One staff member said, "Children would lay down in the hall and tear up the bathroom." Fighting was common.

Parents and students also shared this perception. One parent told us, "My daughter started crying one morning. She didn't want to come to school because she was afraid." Even a student acknowledged, "It wasn't strict enough." In fact, many of the prosperous parents in the immediate neighborhood sent their children to parochial and private schools. Speaking about the community's perception of the school before the current administration, one parent told us, "During the last five to ten years, there has been a huge flight to the private schools."

The school was adrift in terms of leadership. There had been four principals over the course of three years. One staff member said of her first years at Trivette, "I cried every night. I could not function with the way the school functioned then. Nothing prepared me for the first three years." The lack of leadership was noticed by everyone, from community members to teachers to students. "You hardly ever saw the principal. He wasn't at games. He used the same consequences for everything," said a student, speaking about the principal who preceded the current one. "There were lots of behavior problems. Discipline problems. There were concerns about leadership," said a staff member. A teacher said, "There were something like six administrators in two years. One principal was from the central office. He had one year 'til retirement. The old principal would slam the door to his office" rather than deal with situations.

Community members also noticed the problems. "There was fighting all the time. . . . This place had a reputation as a bad school," reported a representative from the local manufacturer. This negative image extended to the local media as well. Stories about fights, disruptions, and academic malfeasance were common. A teacher told us, "In the past, there was lots of negative press. There was a section in the [local newspaper] called 'School News'. There were things like fights or theft. There was negative publicity about the school." In spite of its many successes, this negative public image continues to haunt Trivette.

For the teachers, the lack of leadership and discipline created nothing short of a crisis situation. Beset by unruly students and feeling unsupported by the administration, some teachers began to improvise, finding ways to collaborate and engage in mutual support. To the extent possible, they began working together to devise responses to their predicament. Although these responses were sporadic and lacked formal support, they demonstrate the readiness of the faculty to engage in a change process, even under difficult conditions. Nevertheless, the main result of the constantly changing leadership was that many of the teachers became disillusioned and fulfilled their teaching responsibilities without much enthusiasm. Because student behavior was not exemplary during this tempestuous time, and obedience received more emphasis than enlightenment, very little effort was put into educational reform or restructuring. Trivette was a ship at sea without a captain.

EMBRACING CHALLENGES THROUGH HIDDEN STRENGTHS AND NEW LEADERSHIP

Trivette was beset by several formidable challenges, including a negative image, unstable leadership, and less-than-noteworthy student achievement. Any one of these obstacles would be challenging for a school to overcome. Imagine the potency of the combination of these impediments for a school grounded in traditional standard operating procedures for educating children. A Herculean effort was needed to embrace these challenges and forge them into opportunities for change. As it turned out, Trivette was up to the task. Unnoticed by the casual observer, and certainly by the local media and surrounding community, was an aura of resiliency within the Trivette family that revealed many positive attributes.

On the positive side, the staff was disillusioned but not disinterested, distraught but not disheartened. A teacher described one good outcome of the unstable climate and lack of administrative continuity: "Before (the current administration), we were in limbo. . . . The faculty had to bond to survive. With all that turmoil, our writing scores went up. We have an incredible faculty." Many students continued to achieve despite the disruptive behavior of a growing segment of students. Furthermore, rather than being overwhelmed by discipline problems, the Trivette community chose to interpret them as a wake-up call. Disruptive behavior was viewed by many parents and staff as a sign that changes were needed in traditional methods of teaching and addressing home-school adjustment problems of students. Increasingly, the responsibility for the disruptive behavior in school was shouldered by students, parents, and staff. Another sign of Trivette's strength was that even during these difficult years parent participation was at an acceptable level, although increased participation from minority parents was still needed. Due to these positive aspects of the school, the facilitators were in place to support change. Without leadership at the top, however, these latent strengths were not coordinated and channeled for positive change.

In 1995, the district made a solid commitment to excellence at Trivette Middle by installing as principal Vaughn Deutsch, who was well known and respected in the district as a successful administrator and educator. Deutsch was also a devoted disciple of the Comer SDP and had participated in many hours of training in the Comer philosophy. To further confirm their commitment to Trivette, the district paid for Deutsch to receive additional SDP training from an administrator who enjoyed a national reputation for his knowledge and experience with Comer. This administrator successfully turned around a school that once had a reputation similar to Trivette's.

The stage was now set for a complete reform of Trivette Middle School. A highly respected principal with extensive knowledge of the SDP was assigned to the school. A staff and parent group that had been clamoring for change, any longitudinal change that was comprehensive in scope, was eager for leadership and direction. Support from business and community organizations was waiting to be unbridled. The Comer model, with its emphasis on coordination of instructional and social services and collaboration among parents, children, and teachers, was the appropriate strategy to coalesce all of these forces into action leading to school reform.

INDICATORS OF SUCCESS

From the perspectives of the administration, staff, parents, students, community, and businesses, the changes at Trivette Middle School since Comer implementation have been striking and comprehensive. As evidence of their improvement, members of the Trivette community point to successes in the following areas: school climate, instruction and student achievement, parental involvement, and partnerships.

School Climate

Perhaps the most pronounced success of Trivette Middle School has been a change in the climate of the school. This improved climate, in turn, has started to turn around the school's image in the community. Prior to Comer, Trivette was perceived as a school that was not safe for teachers, parents, or students. Compounding this unfavorable image was the public notion that academic achievement was not a top priority at the school.

Parents, members of the community, and students now consider the school safe. Violent acts by students have decreased dramatically in the last two years. The behavior of Trivette's current seventh graders has improved drastically in comparison with their behavior as incoming sixth graders. Although still disproportionate, suspensions of minority males have been decreasing. With fewer discipline issues to contend with, teachers are able to focus on student achievement. Moreover, the appearance of the school has improved, as the physical plant is well maintained and devoid of graffiti. Consequently, families in the immediate neighborhood have begun sending their children to the school.

The Comer principles of collaboration, consensus, and no fault have been the cornerstone of these successes because they foster a climate of shared responsibility. All individuals involved in the school believe that it has a welcoming atmosphere and makes every effort to engage all interested parties.

Instruction and Student Achievement

According to one teacher, "All students are given a fair shake at Trivette." This claim bespeaks the successful efforts of the Child Assistance Team (CAT) to address the social, emotional, and educational needs of all students. Trivette's increased success in meeting the needs of children at-risk for school failure may certainly be attributed to the no fault and collaboration aspects of the Comer philosophy. The no fault principle has empowered teachers to investigate what works for children rather than identify who or what is to blame for their failure. As a result of the superlative collaborative work of the CAT, many players get involved in making educational modifications to meet the academic challenges of at-risk students.

Another important aspect of Trivette embracing the Comer concepts has been the development of better communication among the teachers, which results in more effective instruction. The school now has teams of teachers who work together. This teaming process has resulted in less isolation and more sharing of ideas. Teaming also facilitates interdisciplinary approaches to teaching. "A concept can carry through all the classes," a teacher told us. Teams also occur at the advisor-advisee level. At this level, the teachers and students talk about issues from home that may affect the learning process. Thus, not only is it possible for instruction to be coordinated, it is possible for teachers to stay better informed about the needs of individual students.

The principle of collaboration enhances the middle school concept of teaming and greatly benefits the instructional program. Teachers are involved in team-teaching activities and confer more frequently on individual student challenges. Furthermore, the SDP has helped expand the definition of the team supporting each student's success. Teachers now see parents as partners in the educational process, communicate with them by phone more frequently, and are more accessible to them when they visit classrooms. This more collaborative approach to supporting academic achievement has led to the following indicators of success: more minority children are on the honor roll, more minority children are in accelerated classes, and academic achievement for minority and majority children has improved and now compares favorably to schools with a higher density of children from middle-class surroundings. Significantly, these indicators show that not only is the overall level of achievement improving, but the distribution of achievement is becoming more equitable.

Parent Involvement

Parent participation among majority parents has always been high at Trivette. However, the participation of minority parents in the school was not at a satisfactory level. Comer has reversed this trend by providing new mechanisms for the school to reach out to all parents and get them involved in the life of the school. Today, it is no longer uncommon to see minority-parents visiting classes and talking with teachers and administrators. Teachers report an increase in minority parent response to solicitations for assistance with students or special projects. A minority parent has been elected to head the PTA for the 1997-98 academic year. According to both staff and community organizations such as the Urban League and NAACP, minority parent participation at Trivette has increased.

All parents feel that since Trivette became a Comer school, they have significant and meaningful new opportunities to serve as volunteers for special projects, both in classrooms and schoolwide. Additionally, the Parent Involvement Team (PIT), in conjunction with the PTA, uses a variety of strategies to encourage parent participation. These include sponsoring fund-raising events, public relations promotions, and recommending selected improvements in the educational program. The PIT increases involvement from communities that are historically underrepresented in school decision making by providing a comfortable forum for the expression of concerns. One African American parent said, "There is more involvement with teachers, and it has helped with the children." Another parent pointed out that, "They have workshops that give us more feel of what's going on in the classrooms. They go out to neighborhoods. It is more community oriented."

Parental involvement is emphasized by the administration, and the main office makes an effort to make parents feel welcome. One parent recalled, "I came in as a parent, and I was amazed by the friendliness. The office said, 'Oh, yes' to me when I wanted to visit." Another parent said, "The school has made a conscientious effort to make parents feel welcome. At the elementary school, we felt welcome. Before the Comer thing here, we didn't."

The improved parent involvement at Trivette goes far beyond what parents perceive as a new climate of openness and friendliness. Parents also expressed satisfaction with the increased access to decision making, and specifically with the kind of decision making that the Comer Process fosters: "The staff strives to make parents feel a part of the decision process and part of the solution. Meetings are structured to be solution oriented, not gripe sessions."

Finally, both teachers and parents report that increased parental involvement has been of great benefit to them and the children. This ownership extends not only to having a real voice in how the school is run, but to knowing what goes on at the school, which in turn has helped improve the school's public image.

Partnerships

Trivette is in the enviable position of being located in close proximity to one of the largest sources of employment in the county, a major textile manufacturer. As part of Trivette's campaign to establish closer ties with the community and get the word out about its turnaround, the school has taken advantage of this proximity by forming a partnership with one of the company's divisions. This has been a very productive partnership on several levels. Members of the company have frequently served as mentors to students and members of parent groups. The company also supports many student academic and social activities by providing school supplies and motivational materials such as T-shirts, caps, and sports equipment. Finally, the company is an integral part of the public relations campaign that resulted in the promotion of Trivette's positive accomplishments within the local community.

Trivette has also formed an assortment of informal community partnerships since becoming a Comer school. Smaller businesses have provided various forms of support for school projects. Many religious institutions within the community have provided support when requested and have served as a reference point regarding the improved reputation of the school. Moreover, social service agencies collaborate with school personnel on home-school related problems.

CONTINUING CHALLENGES

Despite the school's successes, the staff at Trivette still see some challenges before them. A major one is the poor public image that continues to dog them, despite a dramatic decrease in the incidence of violence and disruption and an improvement in academic achievement. Although the growing number of parents and community members who are involved in the school clearly see the changes, Trivette is often still viewed with suspicion by the larger community. Unfortunately, the media continue to publicize outdated negative images. Several staff members recalled an incident that occurred at the high school that shares part of its campus with Trivette. A student there brought a gun to school one day. When the TV crew from the local station arrived to cover the story, it went to Trivette instead of the high school for interviews.

A second continuing challenge is academic achievement. There are improvements, but they have not been dramatic. This area has recently taken on increased prominence in the face of a new state accountability program that carries the threat of financial sanctions, administrative takeover, and public embarrassment. A third area that Trivette continues to pursue is increased minority parent participation. Although it has had success in this area, the school continues to have as one of its goals increasing its reach into the community it serves.

Using the Comer Process, Trivette has already made progress on all of these fronts. The school and its community expect that with their Comer structure they will continue to see improvement in their public image and in minority parent participation. In the area of academic achievement, they plan to implement Padeia and Reading for Real, two programs the staff believe will strengthen Comer's student-centered philosophy at the classroom level.

SUSTAINING THE SUCCESS

The Comer SDP and all of its successes at Trivette are very closely identified with Vaughn Deutsch, the current principal. This raises a crucial question about the future of the reform. If there is another leadership change at the school, can the currently successful Comer program sustain itself? Early interviews with faculty, staff, and parents suggested the possibility that without the presence of Deutsch as a strong Comer advocate, the SDP might languish at Trivette. Thus, it was important for this research to address the question of sustainability. Throughout the three site visits, the investigators were constantly seeking to ascertain the extent to which the success of the SDP could be attributed to the personal factor of the principal as opposed to the implementation of the model itself. During interviews and observations, it was apparent that Comer and Deutsch were viewed synonymously. One teacher indicated, "The school has changed since the principal arrived and started Comer." Another member of the staff exclaimed, "You can't separate Comer from Mr. Deutsch!"

Can the current success of the SDP be sustained at Trivette without the presence of Vaughn Deutsch? Despite the strong role that individual leadership plays in this case, the response is resoundingly affirmative. The majority of the staff believe that Trivette's recent successes may be attributed to the arrival of a supportive principal who advocated for the Comer Process. However, staff and parents agree that the process has now permeated the school's culture and organization so thoroughly that its survival is not dependent on any one individual. In their view, the continuation of Comer's positive momentum at Trivette is assured by three factors. First, there is broad acceptance among staff and parents of the power of the three Comer principles of collaboration, consensus, and no fault. These principles are seen as providing Trivette with the spirit and the mechanism for taking risks to more adequately address the home-school problems of students. Second, the infrastructure of Comer teams is well developed and has led to wide ownership of both school issues and the Comer Process as a means of addressing them. Finally, support for Comer at the district level is another force ensuring the longevity of Comer at Trivette.

A brief history of how the SDP was initiated at Trivette helps to explain the development of these three factors supporting sustainability. The SDP was initiated in Fall 1995 with the arrival of Vaughn Deutsch. Given the low morale of the staff that resulted from the constant change in leaders, it was important for Deutsch to restore their confidence in the building administrator. Deutsch began by listening to their concerns and assuring them of his support and desire to help them change Trivette. As a result of these discussions and Deutsch's manifest commitment toward change, the emphasis of the staff began to shift from behavior management to instruction. The Comer Process was seen as a mechanism that could unite the staff in addressing their shared concerns. "There was an absence of trust here," said the principal, describing the initial situation he faced. "People didn't want to work together, and the Comer Process is so much of that kind of design. We needed to do something. We started talking about building and establishing relationships. Consensus. No voting." This atmosphere created a desire on the part of staff to formulate a clear vision for the school. The principal shared his views on the reform possibilities, and most of the staff indicated a strong interest in adopting the Comer model. Obviously, Deutsch's impressive training in Comer and his passionate belief that the model could address the challenges at Trivette were factors that helped nudge the staff in Comer's direction. Additionally, Deutsch's willingness to support the teachers in a collaborative change process was another major influence in the move toward Comer.

The Trivette staff participated in a variety of SDP workshops and training activities led by the principal. In tandem with these staff-training activities, Deutsch began to engage the community and parents in dialogue about the benefits of Comer. These discussions emphasized the importance of staff, parents, students, and the community participating in a comprehensive plan to change the image and reality of Trivette Middle School. The organizational model and philosophical underpinning for this intense level of collaboration were provided by the SDP.

As the dialogue and training activities continued, the basic organizational structure of Comer was put in place. As described earlier, some of the elements were already in existence, and Comer forged them into a coherent and focused structure. Members were identified for the Comer Parent Involvement Team, Planning and Leadership Team, and Child Assistance Team. In SDP terms, these are the Parent Team, the School Planning and Management Team, and the Student Staff Support Team, respectively. Team membership was determined by volunteers and administrative appointees. The team members believed in the SDP and were strict adherents to the three principles of no fault, consensus, and collaboration. These three principles formed the foundation for the interaction of teams as they began to operate within the framework of the team objectives.

Given this broad and firm foundation, it is easy to see why the Trivette community believes the success of the SDP will be sustained with or without Vaughn Deutsch. The Comer Process provided the dialogue through which the principal, teachers, parents, and community leaders expressed a desire and a willingness to change. This dialogue was conducted within a supportive political climate created by the belief of the district office in Comer. At Trivette it is clear that the Comer principles, infrastructure, and district office support have been and will continue to be the three factors that inspire all efforts to sustain the successes of Comer. A brief discussion of each of these three factors provides further evidence of their importance in supporting and sustaining successful Comer implementation at Trivette.

Guiding Principles

In order for a reform strategy as comprehensive in scope as Comer to be successfully implemented, the culture in which the strategy will operate must be thoroughly examined. Many reform and restructuring initiatives have not been successful because they are simply added to the way schools "do things around here." As a result, these initiatives compete and/or coexist with existing patterns and other initiatives, creating a duplication of effort, overburdening staff, and weakening lines of accountability. The principal and faculty at Trivette were careful to avoid this common blunder. Thus, all existing and new initiatives are embraced under the Comer banner. Initiatives such as Paideia, Reading Renaissance, Reading for Real, Behavior Improvement Center, and tutorial services are all woven into the tapestry of Trivette's Comer Process and implementation of these programs is guided by the core principles.

Implementation of the Comer Process requires that all parties in the school take ownership of the process. According to the SDP, ownership may best be attained by seriously adopting the three principles of consensus, collaboration, and no fault. Deutsch was well aware that the distrust and low morale that existed prior to his arrival could be obstacles to successful Comer implementation. For example, it was difficult for staff to collaborate when blame shifting was running rampant. Also, decision making had been placed in the hands of a select few, a policy that did little to improve morale.

It was through the process of collaboration and consensus that the principal, faculty, and parents agreed on a need for change. According to Deutsch, this was a valuable insight because without genuine recognition of the need for change, no one has any incentive to take risks. Collaboration and consensus principles are not easily adopted without appropriate give and take. They require bonds of trust between all parties to the decision process. However, once everyone in the school community agreed that if Trivette was to improve some change would be required on all of their parts, the culture of the school could be reshaped.

The reshaping of the culture was propelled by the no fault principle. In essence, our interviews revealed that this principle permitted everyone to focus on meeting the needs of children, rather than engaging in retrenchment, recrimination, and blame. As one staff member stated, once the no fault principle was adopted, "The focus of the discussion was on what we are going to do now, rather than what we did before." Faculty and parents are quite comfortable with the three principles and cannot imagine returning to the previous form of communication and accountability. With faith in the three principles as a guidepost, the leadership issue, although important, will not greatly influence efforts to sustain the Comer Process at Trivette Middle School.

Infrastructure

Prior to Comer, teachers and staff at Trivette operated independently of one another, each going about his or her own business. Under this mode of operation, accountability for instruction was weak, children at-risk for school failure fell through the cracks, and the sense of a learning community was nonexistent. The Comer team structure has motivated the teachers to work together to examine issues on the basis of what is good for the school, as well as the individual students. Working together in teams has also had an impact on the school's culture and strengthened resolve to sustain the successes gained by the Comer Process.

Within the SDP structure at Trivette Middle School, there are three teams: Planning and Leadership Team (PLT), Child Assistance Team Services (CATS), and Parent Involvement Team (PIT). The teams are the most visible aspect of Comer at the school, and, along with the decision-making principles that guide their work, drive most of Trivette's success.

The PLT, the leadership arm of the team concept, oversees budget planning, monitors the school improvement plan, addresses teacher and parent concerns, and assists in the formulation and implementation of school policy. "We oversee all functions of the school. Budget, recommendations for things. All major decisions come through here," one team member told us. Two serious issues for the team have been the budget and plans for improving achievement. As with any organization, allocation of resources can be a contentious issue. One team member explained, "Money is allocated for each department. Each department has to decide how to use the money."

The CATS team is responsible for addressing student academic, social, and behavioral concerns. This team provides a perfect example of the success of the student-centered approach. This multidisciplinary team exerts every effort to design educational solutions that promote inclusion rather than exclusion of struggling students. For this to take place, the entire staff had to adopt an inclusive school philosophy that embraces and celebrates all forms of diversity—ethnicity, disabilities, and socioeconomic status, for example. Consequently, maintaining and supporting the inclusive nature of the educational programs is perceived as a shared responsibility.

The PIT is responsible for ensuring that parents are a part of the instructional process. This means involving parents at every level of school activity from policy formulation to classroom implementation. Faculty and parents support this team as a legitimate method of garnering stakeholder support and ownership for Trivette Middle School's total program. The PIT concept facilitates parents' efforts to address common educational issues. This team also provides a very healthy public relations function because the parents get first-hand information about school operations and, in turn, this information flow influences their roles as goodwill ambassadors. Although Trivette is still working to increase minority parent participation, the PIT has become an integral part of the Trivette school culture. Parents are unlikely to willingly relinquish their high visibility should a change in principal result in a more autocratic, hierarchical leader.

The decisions of all teams are made with the developmental pathways in mind, whether they are planning for school-wide events or dealing with an individual child. "The pathways run through your mind before you do something. They let us be more accepting of behaviors and give us a chance to work with the student," said a teacher on the PLT.

The examples presented clearly illustrate how the Comer team concept has been successful in reshaping the culture of the school. Prior to Comer, teachers and staff operated independently of one another and parents were largely unheard in school decision making. Today, working together in teams that use the guiding principles, all members of the Trivette community are united in their focus on school improvement. The Comer Process has made Trivette a community of learners to the extent that Deutsch is seen as just another learner and teacher. Should Deutsch exit, the community will utilize the team structure to sustain their positive momentum.

District Support

This firm foundation of support for Comer at the school level is buttressed by top-level support from the superintendent and school board. This strategic level of support can promote the longevity of the program through administrative assignments, resource allocations, and district-supported growth activities related to Comer. In Vaughn Deutsch's case, the superintendent and the board used an administrative appointment to initiate the change toward Comer. A similar action could be taken if Deutsch leaves. Comer schools in this district enjoy a respectable level of resources, and this is a high motivational factor for the staff to continue using Comer.

Administrative appointments and resources aside, Trivette staff and parents believe in the Comer Process. They understand how it operates to strengthen the bond between home and school in educating children. They have seen the power that Comer brings to efforts to improve schools through a child-centered approach. In addition, staff and parents appreciate the SDP as a tool of empowerment that enables them to take risks in charting their course for continually improving the school's educational program.

CONCLUSION

Perhaps the most powerful lesson to be learned from Trivette is that successful school reform is more apt to take place if the principal advocates some form of structured change. It is equally important that teachers and parents acknowledge the need for and are willing to participate as full partners in this change. The Comer Process at Trivette is still strongly identified with the principal who was its forceful initial advocate ("Mr. Deutsch is Comer"). Yet, today the process is thoroughly integrated into the structure and culture of the school and strongly supported at the district level. Leadership was critical to initiating the Comer Process and continues to play an important role, but the success experienced by Trivette will have to be sustained by the entire school community. Working together in teams and guided by the principles of consensus, collaboration, and no fault, the administration, staff, and parents of Trivette will continue to use Comer as a powerful tool for improvement focused on the needs of children.

6

West High School

Carol E. Malloy
University of North Carolina at Chapel Hill

Jean A. Patterson
Wichita State University

After the last bus has left at the end of another school day and another school week, Principal Janice Sawyer sinks into her office chair and exhales a deep sigh. A tall, thin woman whose angular features are softened by the curve of her smile, Ms. Sawyer is the embodiment of an energetic, dedicated school administrator. During this brief moment, however, her weariness is evident. She tells us that she has the highest staff turnover rate as well as the most inexperienced teachers in the system's high schools. Despite its recent success, the school's location on "the wrong side of town" and a lingering reputation for poor performance make it difficult to attract and hold on to teachers. At least 40% of the current faculty have less than three years teaching experience, and 22 of the 100 faculty members are leaving at the end of the 1996-97 school year. Unable to convince many teachers to even come to West for an interview, she is having a difficult time recruiting new faculty members.

West High School presently enrolls 1,500 students in grades 9-12, with approximately 53% African American, 45% white, and 2% Asian and Latino students. A significant percentage of the students are considered "at risk" for poor performance or dropping out. The students have complex problems, and the challenges for teachers in reaching them are often not purely academic, but social and emotional. The teaching staff is 33% African American and 25% male. There are many new programs Principal Sawyer would like to add, but instead she must manage the loss of four academic positions while trying to maintain current programs. We ask her how is it possible to sustain this level of commitment given the odds against the school. She shakes her head and says she does not know, but something will have to give because the community will not settle for failure or retrenchment.

In the face of these seemingly insurmountable obstacles, Ms. Sawyer holds steadfast to her faith in the Comer Process to help the school and the community collectively face their difficult circumstances. She firmly believes that "Comer saved us—Comer saved this school," and that the Comer Process is crucial to the school's ongoing struggle for survival.

When you walk into West High at the start of the school day, you see a school that is clean, brightly lit, and full of life. On the outside, parents drop off students at the door where they quickly greet their friends and begin the school day. The office staff are busy dealing with students, and the principal is handling the concerns of students, teachers, and visitors alike. By the time the last bell rings, the halls are clear and students seem ready to begin their school day.

From this glimpse, all seems well at West High. On the surface, it is not apparent how hard the students and staff of West High have worked to survive as a school with a successful educational program. It is not apparent that someone in the community calls the media every time there is a minor disturbance at the school. It is not apparent that in recent years changes occurred that would normally devastate a school, such as dramatic and unsettling changes in student population, principals, and teachers. None of this is immediately apparent because the school has survived and continues to persevere.

However, there are many positive things about West High that are readily apparent. West High is a Comer school. The hallways, offices, and classroom doors announce Comer principles. The students, who seem pleased to be a part of the school, come from diverse backgrounds. Teachers and counselors have smiles on their faces and greet students who have questions. This school seems to be a happy place to learn and to teach.

This case study describes how West High has used the Comer Process and its own internal resources to navigate a number of difficult transitions. Section II discusses how the shifting demographics of the school's community confronted the school with new challenges. Section III describes how West High and its new leaders used the Comer Process to revitalize the school. Section IV presents the details of West's comprehensive school development plan and describes its team structure. Section V provides evidence of the school's successes since Comer implementation. Section VI presents some dissenting views on how effective Comer has been at West, suggesting some areas where the school may need to shore up the process. Section VII summarizes West High's Comer implementation and future direction.

SHIFTING DEMOGRAPHICS, SHIFTING PROBLEMS

When West High School opened its doors in 1951 as a comprehensive high school, its rural location was far removed from the reaches of city life. The students were the sons and daughters of farmers, laborers, and other working-class people. To this day the close-knit community is fiercely proud and protective of its school. Every spring the community joins with West to raise money by sponsoring a barbecue. The event becomes an all-night social gathering that parents, faculty, and students eagerly anticipate. Alumni and former employees from 20 to 30 years past return for this annual event, which has taken on a life of its own. No longer just a school function, the annual barbecue is more about the community than it is about the school. The high school's many traditions run deep and are kept alive by successive generations of sons and daughters who take their parents' places at the school.

As the city began to encroach on the school's pastoral setting, West was faced with new challenges. Urbanization and desegregation brought a more diverse group of students into the school. In spite of strong community support, West High became entrenched in the public's consciousness as a low-performing high school. With the business and housing markets expanding into southern and eastern locations in the county, the "west side," ever the bastion of blue-collar workers, was perceived as the "wrong side of town." The growth of the nearby airport into an international transportation hub resulted in the constant presence of commercial airplanes in the sky over the school. Even with the school's stability and proud traditions, the teachers, students, and parents of West High were not immune to the perception that they were a second-class school because the community was located on the wrong side of the town. Their neighborhood and school were in the western part of the county where working class people lived. There were no doctors' children. The racially diverse population of students represented regular people with parents who scratched out a living in middle-level jobs.

West High was already a school with a shaky image when in 1992 a change in school district policy dramatically altered the historically stable student population. The reconstitution of nearby Edison High School played a central role in determining the direction West High School eventually would take. Edison served a predominantly low-income student population and was viewed by the district and the community as "dysfunctional" in terms of academic success, management of the school, and the large number of severe behavior problems. In Spring 1992, Edison was closed as a neighborhood school and reopened that Fall as a magnet program that emphasized math, science, and technology. Although this was a positive new start for Edison, it had serious negative repercussions for West High. To make room for Edison's magnet program, 400 of their more difficult students were reassigned to West, which drastically altered the make-up of the school's clientele. According to an assistant principal at West, 140 of the 141 ninth and tenth graders who came from Edison that year had at least one failing grade on their report card. Forty-three of the ninth graders had already repeated ninth grade at least twice. Thus, whereas the math, science, and technology magnet program revitalized Edison High School, the problems were not resolved, but merely shifted to West.

The school district probably believed that the traditions of West High were strong enough to sustain this shift in population, but it was devastating. West was already struggling with poor academic achievement, lowered teacher morale, safety issues, and an overall bad public image. The teachers had not lost control of the educational programs in the school, but they did not have the kind of control they felt they needed. In addition to bringing in a large new group of challenging students, the magnet program also "creamed off" West's best and brightest students. This left the school with a disproportionately large population of at-risk students. Teachers stated that after the shift, "we not only had the crunch of a school that's in a low-middle class area, but we took a hit with our academics and our students' achievement scores tumbled." Teachers felt powerless to say that they did not want these new students in their school. They felt that they had become a magnet school dump site.

Tensions among the old community and the large block of newcomers created an unsettling environment that was divisive and conflictual and occasionally exploded into violence. Old-line West parents, despite their devotion, grew fearful of sending their children to the school. The current principal described West as "a combination of generations of families and a transient population." The once predominantly white student body had also gradually shifted to a majority-minority student population. The community, parents, faculty, staff, and students felt that they were in danger of losing the West High they once knew. To work through this difficult transition, the school staff had to look more carefully at the school's organization and the instructional program offered to the students. With the arrival of a new principal, the Comer Process became the mechanism for carrying out this much-needed overhaul.

TAKING BACK OUR SCHOOL WITH THE COMER PROCESS

"We took back our school with the Comer Process. We used to have drugs, violence—the police were here more often than parents."—West High parent

"Sometimes it's hard to know what was Comer and what was Dr. Thompson."—West High teacher

By Spring of 1992, West High had few success stories. The school was in a state of inertia. Students were not achieving at adequate levels, teacher and staff morale was low, teacher turnover was at an all-time high, and parental participation was nonexistent except for the annual community barbecue. The impact of the transferred students from Edison High weighed heavily on the instructional and social programs of the school. Decision making was strictly top-down, and teachers felt that they had no voice in school policymaking. Teachers retreated into their classrooms, supporting each other as best they could, but paid little heed to school-wide issues over which they had little control. They said, "we took care of one another because they [the administration] did not take care of us." West High was in desperate need of direction and strong leadership.

In Summer 1992, the teachers read about their new leader and his plans to implement the Comer model at West High. Weary and skeptical after all the changes they had been through, their first impression was that this was just "one more program to be implemented" that ultimately would have little impact on the school's pressing needs. There was further apprehension when they met Dr. Thompson because he was "so young" and had no experience in a high school. Teachers simply did not have much faith that this principal and his program would make a difference in their school.

Dr. Michael Thompson, a dynamic, energetic principal, was brought to West High specifically to take on the challenges of leading a school that was in transition. Individuals described the school at that point in time as "stagnant," "fragmented," and "drowning and not going anywhere." Thompson related what he encountered on arriving at West High School:

> Here's a high school that's already struggling to promote itself as a place of academic excellence. In fact, the community was disenchanted with the school, the teachers were at a point of giving up on themselves and subsequently the students, and then to have 500 additional students to be added to the enrollment that had their major problems also was a real blow to the school. That was the setting that I walked into in 1992.

Because he saw a school in crisis, Thompson decided that implementation of Comer at West would initially have to be more principal-driven than collaborative. As a manager, Thompson described himself as "one who had a hammer in one hand and a carrot in the other." He experienced considerable tension between the need to immediately address the school's critical state and his desire to develop the talents of others and to facilitate shared decision making. Thompson attempted to maintain a delicate balance between his own high expectations and tough standards and his efforts to nurture relationships and inspire students and teachers to expect more from themselves. However, he emphasizes that he never strayed from his ultimate goal of having the Comer Process become collaborative and draw on the collective wisdom of the faculty.

Nearly everyone associated with West recognized the need for significant change. This recognition is a necessary first step. However, in a school that was unaccustomed to leadership changes over the years, the faculty was particularly apprehensive about this unknown young principal. Realizing that he would have to establish credibility and gain the support of the teachers and the community, Dr. Thompson deliberately chose not to introduce the Comer Process as "just another program" dictated from the top. Instead, he began to implement Comer principles by example. One teacher's comment about the subtleties of the "Comerization" process was echoed by others: "I don't remember being Comerized. I just remember we were all of a sudden." Cognizant that people were "tired of educational rhetoric," Dr. Thompson believed that it was important to spend his time *doing* Comer rather than just *talking* about Comer. When Thompson did formally introduce the process, teachers were familiar with its basic tenets and already involved in the decision-making processes.

Even after carefully laying the groundwork, Thompson still faced considerable resistance from those faculty members who were unwilling to let go of traditional ways of thinking about how schools should be organized and operated. He sympathized with their skepticism given that many of these teachers were accustomed to seeing reform efforts come and go with limited benefit to the students. All he asked for was the benefit of the doubt. Many of these teachers adopted a "wait and see" attitude toward the changes Thompson was proposing. There were some, however, who were simply unwilling to change their thinking about the way schools should be managed or critically examine their teaching practices as the Comer Process required. These teachers were encouraged to transfer or retire. Although most faculty members eventually came to support the Comer Process, the school still experienced the loss of half of its faculty and staff during the first two years of implementation.

Empowering faculty, staff, students, and parents by giving them a voice in decision making is a cornerstone of the Comer philosophy. However, in educational reform, the rhetoric of empowerment is all too often used without substantive changes taking place in existing power arrangements, with the principal continuing to make the major decisions. Thompson was sensitive to the faculty's initial distrust that he would conduct himself any differently and actually broaden access to meaningful decision making authority. The comments of an assistant principal are indicative of these pervasive concerns when Thompson first arrived at West:

> I think trust was the biggest issue. I don't think people really trusted Michael when he first got here. . . . It took a long time to understand that [Comer] was not a program, that it was more [of] a process. . . . I don't think we trusted that our school planning was going to be able to make decisions. Everybody always had a principal that made every decision. I think the issue was "Why is it going to be any different with this guy?"

Thus, it was even more important that the Comer principles of no fault, consensus building, and collaborative leadership be faithfully enacted in practice. Thompson noted the power of action over rhetoric:

Over time as we demonstrated that we were serious about the faithful repli-
cation of the process and that we were not just giving lip service to this
notion of consensus building, collaborative leadership, and the no fault
principle, more and more people began to catch the vision that I kept presenting. And over time we were able to develop a critical mass of people
who believed in what we were doing. When that happened, we began to see
a major change in the school.

Slowly but deliberately, Dr. Thompson convinced the staff that change
was possible. He made the teachers into believers by listening to their concerns
about having a room where they could work together and then by acting to
change one of the unused classroom suites into a teachers' lounge. At the same
time, Dr. Thompson selected key staff members who were committed to change
and asked them to facilitate the move to the Comer Process.

Dr. Thompson remained at West High during the first three years of
Comer implementation. Most educational initiatives live and die with the principals who initiate them, but by the time Thompson left West High, Comer was
embedded in the school's culture. The Comer Process had become a way of life
for the administration, faculty, and students, and the Comer principles under-
pinned the way decisions were made throughout the school. Furthermore,
Thompson's successor, Janice Sawyer, had worked with him as an assistant
principal and was committed to sustaining the Comer Process.

Ms. Sawyer has ensured the continuation of the Comer Process at West
High, although very much in her own way. Whereas Thompson was a beacon of
light, leading the way for Comer implementation, Ms. Sawyer is a steadying
influence who sees that the school stays on the Comer course. As buy-in to the
process broadens and deepens in the school community, Ms. Sawyer believes
that the most valuable leadership role is one of facilitation and support. Like her
predecessor, she also understands the value of action and relationships over
rhetoric. According to an assistant principal, "She's accessible to teachers, has
an open door." Even at West High, with its complex problems and the many
demands placed on her, Ms. Sawyer still manages to find time for her faculty
and staff. These relationships extend beyond the teaching staff to include those
not directly involved in the instructional programs. Regardless of their roles at
West High, each staff member feels valued and has an important role in using
the Comer Process to focus the school on the needs of students. This inclusiveness was exemplified by a security guard who commented, "I like working with
Ms. Sawyer and the Comer Process and the idea of looking at the whole child.
She listens to my ideas."

WEST HIGH'S COMPREHENSIVE SCHOOL DEVELOPMENT PLAN

The central manifestation of West High's Comer implementation is its Comprehensive School Development Plan (SDP). Collectively, faculty, administration, parents, and students strongly believe in the SDP and describe it as a "living document." The plan, which drives the school program, is the product of an ongoing dialogue about the school's needs and what must be done to meet them. This dialogue is conducted using the Comer principles of consensus, collaboration, and no fault. Teachers called the SDP an amazing document.

West High explains its commitment to the Comer Process in a general information document that details the history and future of the Comer Process in the school. The document describes the first year of implementation as having "ups and downs" because of the stress related to change in governance. The document also states that positive changes in school climate enabled staff to build momentum for the implementation strategies used in the following school year.

These initial implementation strategies required the entire staff to participate in both the planning and execution of change. Within the school, staff aligned the instructional program with the needs of the students. The internal resources of the school were also aligned with community resources to support the instructional program. The four areas of focus were: strategic planning, instructional program, school climate and social development, and school communications. Once change strategies were developed through a process of consensus and collaboration, the mechanisms through which change was realized were embodied in the teams that created the SDP.

The SDP in place at West High consists of four major teams or committees: the School Planning and Management Team (SPMT), which plans and coordinates school activities; the Student and Services Management Team (SSMT), which intervenes and provides services for at-risk students who are experiencing problems or barriers to learning; the Instructional Advisory Committee (IAC), an adaptation of the Comer model specific to West High that plans school-wide instructional programs and mediates instructional and curricular issues with the SPMT; and the Parent Team (PT), which involves parents in school activities. The interrelated nature of the teams and committees is diagrammed in Figure 6.1.

The work of these teams and of West High's Comer Process is generally carried out using the three guiding principles of no fault, consensus, and collaboration. As described in Comer literature, *no fault* focuses on the work that must be accomplished and on providing nonjudgmental feedback rather than assigning blame for what has already occurred. *Consensus* is a slow, convergent process in which diverse voices are empowered and heard, as opposed to a speedy, linear process in which the exercise of power leads to paralysis.

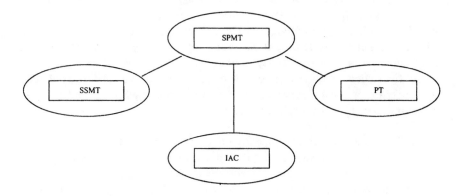

Figure 6.1. West High School's Teams and Committees

Collaboration means promoting interdependence, integration, and coordination of efforts over independence and fragmentation. In explaining how the principles are related, the staff focuses on *no fault* as a philosophy for working with students and trying novel approaches in their instruction. *Consensus* and *collaboration* are viewed as the communication standard for making decisions that will benefit the students and the school. Each of the four teams uses these principles to carry out their part in the SDP. The four teams and their missions are described next.

SPMT

Teachers, counselors, administrators, and the principal are members of this team, which meets once a week or as needed. SPMT members are elected by the school-at-large for three year terms, with one third of the members elected each year. Thus, membership changes from year to year. Two co-chairs, not the principal, develop the agenda and lead the meetings. The SPMT is responsible for the day-to-day operations of the school, including school-wide policies, staff concerns, calendars, departmental information, and other issues that involve students. Several members of the IAC and the SSMT are also members of this team. Comer parents, students, and support staff participate in the extended SPMT that meets once a month. The overlapping membership of the teams facilitates integrated dialogue among teams and committees.

SSMT

The SSMT is an interdisciplinary team of teachers, counselors, and support personnel whose purpose is to identify at-risk students and help them achieve success in school. The West High model integrates and incorporates the functions of the typical Comer Student Services Support Team (SSST) with the Assistance Team, a group already in place at West that served as a prereferral group for students with academic problems. The mandated school-based committee for exceptional children remains separate from the SSMT but has representation on it. The team explained that this model:

- provides more direct student services with less duplication;
- provides collaboration with administration, student services, classroom instruction, parental involvement, and community resources;
- allows for early identification of at-risk students and reduction in the number of students referred for in-school and out-of-school suspension;
- reduces student absences and the drop-out rate;
- increases the number of family interventions and appropriate follow up; and
- increases the number of services provided for at-risk students.

The team meets once a week to discuss student referrals, support services, connections with parents and outside agencies, and other issues confronting students. Consistent with an interdisciplinary approach, the SSMT uses a mailbox system for the identification of issues. They accept student referrals only after classroom interventions have taken place. Beyond their core work with individual students, the team felt that their most successful school-wide accomplishments were the implementation of literacy and sexual harassment programs. Team members explained that they used the Comer Process to identify the need for these two programs and implemented them with the help of the SPMT and the IAC. When the SSMT identified a need for these programs at West High, they first went to the SPMT for a policy decision and then to community resources and the IAC for the educational components.

As with all the teams, the guiding principles appear to be the foundation of this team's work. Team members stated that the avoidance of finding fault or placing blame increased collective responsibility and accountability for student learning. One member said, "We all accept responsibility. There is some reason why that child is not learning—that's why. We were put together to find out why." The process allows the needs of the students to be identified and helps students and staff find the necessary assistance. Team members stated that the principle of collaboration is crucial to connecting students with resources because it removes the barriers of departments and reduces "turf" disputes.

They argue that since Comer was instituted, the staff is more focused and expectations are clearly understood. As evidence of this, they point to increased dialogue across departments and areas, the diminished need for "power" cliques among the faculty, and the support provided for new teachers: "The staff feels that they are working together."

The SSMT reported that the only drawback of the Comer Process is the time that is required for meetings. However, they emphasize that they will continue to take the time because the process makes everyone feel that they are a part of the school and, most importantly, that the center of the school is the children and their families.

IAC

The Comer Process focuses attention on six developmental pathways for student growth: cognitive, physical, language, psychological, ethical, and social. The structure of the Comer Process does not designate direct responsibility for these pathways. West High created the Instructional Advisory Committee to ensure that the school's Comer planning process attends to the pathways. The mission of the IAC is to facilitate a sound instructional program with optimal educational opportunities for all students. The committee provides instructional leadership to the principal regarding personnel, instructional scheduling, curriculum assistance, instructional resources, and communications. More specifically, the IAC has been involved in instructional matters such as curriculum alignment, support of teachers based on assessment data, new courses to reduce gaps in the curriculum, course registration and participation, changes in scheduling, inclusion, and support for students who are having difficulty.

Department chairs and administrators, who form the committee, meet with other chairs once or twice a month as needed to discuss instructional decisions. The principal develops the agenda for the meetings, and department chairs merge their issues into the agenda. Faculty and staff issues are brought to the IAC after first being discussed in department meetings. If consensus is reached in departments on issues to be placed on the IAC agenda, then the department chair acts as the agent/advocate for the department in bringing the issue to the IAC. Although the SPMT and IAC have related mandates, West High faculty articulate their distinct roles. Most teachers clearly believe that the mandate of the IAC is curricular, whereas the SPMT handles policy. As an example of this distinction, they noted that when the exam schedule did not provide enough time for instruction, the IAC proposed new dates for the testing. Because this required a change in policy, the final approval came from SPMT.

Members of the IAC feel that they have made significant contributions in supporting student achievement and reducing multiple repeaters in courses. In order to ensure that student needs are addressed, the IAC investigated innovative programs throughout the school district. Within West High, they profiled each department to determine its strengths and weaknesses and used this data to formulate strategies to improve student results on end-of-course tests, to help the school meet system-mandated benchmark goals, and to enable teachers to improve their instruction. Guidance data, PSAT scores, and grade histories were used to recruit students who otherwise might not have been recommended into upper level courses.

PT

The Parent Team members live in all areas of the large attendance zone and are united in their focus on improving West High and supporting the school's programs. A few of these parents are also teachers in the school. These parents understand that it is their responsibility to be supportive of the school's instructional and civic programs. They spoke highly of the administration and praised the counselors for "recruiting students to be more productive and challenged even when they are in classes with students who are at-risk." They think that the Comer Process has gotten parents on the same "wave length" as the teachers and described the faculty by saying, "They get along with the kids. Teachers are happy to be here and participate in many extra activities."

Parents on the PT cited dramatic increases in openness and parent participation as evidence of how the school has changed through the Comer Process: "The school is more open, they ask for more volunteers, and we have more input." They also felt that they had more contact with the administration and that they could "walk into the school at any time. If there is a problem, they will not whitewash it." West's long-standing tradition of parent-community ownership, shored up by Comer during a transition period, is exemplified by the frequent comment, "This is our school, too." Parents have also noticed changes in their children's participation in school activities and decision making and appreciated their children asking them to be more involved. One parent stated:

> My daughter is more open to talk to me about what is going on in school. She even will go to the principal and talk about her concerns. She has gotten me more involved. The students in the community know us. She said, "My dad is more popular (in school) than I am."

These Comer parents believe that "when the school calls you, it's your civic responsibility to respond." This attitude undergirds the role of West High's PT in the school's improvement process.

Comer Subcommittees

Although most of the planning is done by the four Comer teams just described, the entire staff responds to the SDP as members of 13 active subcommittees that address many areas of the school program including staff development, research and assessment, public relations, incentives, technology, multiculturalism, and social events. Every professional staff member is assigned to a committee. These professionals take their membership seriously because they believe their input is important to the total school program.

The commitment to help West High achieve success can be heard in the voices of teachers as they describe the "endless meetings." Teachers individually and collectively stated, "We meet a lot." There are scheduled after-school meetings for committees, departments, and the full faculty 3 of the 4 Wednesdays in the month. Additionally, teachers who are on one of the four Comer teams meet regularly during the school day. But as they roll their eyes about the hectic meeting schedule, they smile, because the Comer Process has made the school "a different environment, friendly, no blame, supportive, and cohesive."

West High views the Comer Process as a governance structure that brings coherence to the educational, social, and political aspects of school life. All of the school's efforts to meet students' needs take place within this framework. For example, because of the geographic, ethnic, and socioeconomic diversity of the student body, the school has instituted several programs that directly support student achievement:

- Civic responsibility, which teaches civic and social responsibility through U.S. history (students have to commit five hours to community service and write a paper on the experience);
- Indian express, an incentive program that recognizes and rewards students' academic efforts and achievements;
- Character education, which concentrates on student interaction in relation to life in the school; and
- Writing across the curriculum, which concentrates on student research within content areas based on a model established by the English department.

All of these programs touch in different ways on the diverse student needs highlighted by Comer's developmental pathways.

SHARING THE VISION: COMER SUCCESSES

"The biggest thing, which is an intangible, is that the school has hope again."
—Dr. Michael Thompson, former principal

Those associated with West High relate the school's survival through rocky times and its ongoing transformation directly to the Comer Process. A common thread running through these successes is that Comer has created a support system for faculty, staff, and parents and woven a safety net around students. Because of their active participation in the Comer Process, faculty members no longer feel isolated or helpless when problems arise. Parents now feel more comfortable visiting the school, as they no longer feel excluded or alienated. Administrators, teachers, support staff, and parents alike believe that they are an integral part of the West High community.

Using Comer's guiding principles and developmental pathways has also contributed to an understanding that every student is the responsibility of the collective. This becomes particularly evident when parents are no longer solely concerned with their own children's needs. One parent's comment aptly captures this insight: "You can be an active parent in a child's life. Not just your child, but other children, too. Children are everybody's responsibility. I'm an active participant in every child's education."

The principal describes the teachers as focused, student-oriented, committed, and close-knit, much like a family. Her view is that they are receptive to new ideas, have a global perspective on teaching and learning, and have high values and expectations for student achievement. Counselors described the teachers as "the most hard working staff you will ever meet. You will not find anyone who does not pull their weight." Teachers and students also described the staff in similar words.

The majority of the students interviewed believed that their teachers cared about them, were concerned for their safety, and wanted them to do well in school. These students also recognized that graduation from high school, to higher education, and their future goals were important to the school.

Comer Empowers Those Usually Without Power: Teachers, Parents, Students

The Comer principles of collaborative leadership and consensus building require changes in the hierarchical power relationships that typically exist in schools. The role of the principal in a Comer school is significantly different from the traditional authority figure. As former principal Thompson related, "The principal becomes more of an instructional leader, more of a facilitator, a developer, a person who influences decisions as opposed to making decisions." Not surprisingly, current principal Sawyer described herself in similar terms: "I'm a curriculum and instructional leader, not a manager."

At West High, teachers and parents consistently indicated that they were involved in making decisions and well-informed about the issues affecting the school. They believed that their input was genuine and valued. This perspective is exemplified by this parent's comment: "Faculty and administration ask your opinion and don't discard your opinion. They take our advice, they don't dictate to us." A teacher shared a similar sentiment: "I feel that my opinion is more valued at this Comer school. I'm asked my opinion several times over several issues and it's not taken lightly."

Parents also described improved communication and more positive relationships with West High's administrative staff. They believe that the administration is more accessible to them, more honest, and more willing to tackle the school's tough issues than before West High became a Comer school.

Teachers who had worked in other settings expressed a noticeable difference between their past experiences and the environment at West High today. A teacher new to West High described the process with admiration: "They have a committee to deal with everything. In other schools, things went directly to the principal." Another new teacher noted that "faculty meetings are open-people feel safe about saying something and raising issues without fear."

In implementing Comer at the high school level, efforts have also been made to include students in decision-making processes, primarily through surveys. Ms. Sawyer also holds weekly student forums at which about 12 students join her for lunch to discuss their concerns and issues. A smaller number of students attend the extended SPMT. Most faculty members believe that the opportunities West High provides for student participation have contributed to the school's success. One teacher observed, "I think the students feel they have a say-so in some of the things that go on in the school and that helps us be successful also." A member of the support staff also noted, "You can tell there's a different atmosphere here. The students have access to the office and administration. You don't see that in most high schools." Most students interviewed also felt that they had a voice in the school and that the administration and faculty truly listened to them, as the comments of these students attest:

> I think the Comer Process makes a lot of students feel good, though. Because I know when I can voice my opinion, since we are the ones who deal with it every day and we're the ones it effects, I think it gives you that good feeling that, hey, they are listening to me or they are trying to, and not ignoring.

> They want to hear our opinion of what we have to say about this certain situation. They want to hear that and not just walk on. Whatever is inside, they want to hear it.

Comer Decisions Get Things Done

West High faculty, staff, and students believe that they are empowered because they see their collective decisions put into practice. Comer is dependent on team processes, on people taking the time to meet and talk with each other. Every faculty member serves on a least one committee and most serve on several. Although the amount of time devoted to participating on committees was a commonly identified concern, no one felt that these meetings were a waste of time. As one teacher explained: "We do see results, it's not just meetings with nothing being accomplished out of those meetings." This perspective was further reinforced by a teacher's account of what happened at a recent faculty meeting when Ms. Sawyer announced that she was seeking volunteers to serve on two more committees:

> Everybody laughed because there are so many committees and people are all working so hard and everybody's committed to several things. Then she said, "Let me describe them to you." She described the committees and hands shot up. There was no problem filling those committees.

Similarly, when problems do arise, the Comer teams are a functional mechanism through which problems can be discussed and resolved. As another teacher related, "We do take action and we do work as quickly as possible to find solutions to problems and to implement those solutions." The Comer teams at West High also seem to effectively prevent most issues from becoming isolated or departmentalized. Curiously, although a few individuals indicated that the Comer team process of discussing issues and obtaining consensus was slow, deliberate, and inefficient, most believed that these processes actually facilitated quicker and more immediate responses to the school's concerns and issues.

Researchers observed an example of how the Comer structure facilitates responsiveness to emerging issues. In Spring 1997, the SPMT was reviewing the newly implemented decision to change from one to two lunch periods. Problems with overcrowding, discipline, and cleanliness prompted the original decision. During a special meeting of the SPMT, the staff reviewed the results of the decision and found that the lunch periods were calmer, the cafeteria was much cleaner, and teachers and parents were pleased. Many students, however, were not pleased. The SPMT was interested in conducting a more comprehensive and organized evaluation of the change. The principal suggested an informal survey of teachers and students. The Team decided immediately to survey the teachers and informally survey selected students during the following week. Two members agreed to develop the surveys. They discovered that students were unhappy because they might now be in different lunch periods than their friends. Moreover, students, counselors, and teachers were all concerned about the tutoring and club meetings that had always occurred during the lunch hours. The team quickly suggested that it was possible to modify the lunch schedule on Fridays to accommodate the clubs, and they are still analyzing additional accommodations for tutoring during the lunch periods.

Comer Provides a Support System for Faculty and a Safety Net for Students

In most large high schools, faculty and staff typically turn to their departments or other small groups of friends and colleagues for support. Factions, cliques, and coalitions typically form to promote shared interests or to defend against perceived threats. However, at West High, faculty members spoke of a cohesive, supportive administrative and teaching staff. Faculty loyalties are aligned with the school as a whole rather than with a department or other subgroup. Teachers asserted that they believe most West High faculty and staff place the interests of the school and students ahead of personal or departmental agendas:

> I think everyone is willing to give up . . . their own needs or wants at school for the good of the whole. I think a lot of people are willing to sacrifice their individual preferences for school safety, or things that will benefit the entire school in general.

In fact, West High faculty and staff insisted that there are no factions or cliques among them. Teachers interviewed felt that they were on equal footing with everyone else and had no need to shore up a power base by establishing coalitions. A veteran teacher who is new to West High this year commented on the striking absence of favoritism or a privileged elite: "In my walk through life, I didn't always have the opportunity, but here the opportunity exists for teachers to head committees and become department chairs. In other situations, the opportunities weren't there." The Comer team structure is one important source of this faculty cohesiveness. Because they bring together representatives of the various departments and other constituents to examine and resolve issues, Comer teams have eliminated many of the reasons that prompt factions, cliques, and coalitions to emerge. With this support system in place, teachers do not feel isolated or alone when confronting the difficulties of teaching a largely at-risk student population. This teacher articulates the importance of this unity and support to her work:

> God, if I were by myself. . . . This school would be a nightmare if I had to do this all by myself. I would be completely clueless and without any support and I just couldn't do that and teach at this school.

In addition to serving as a support system for faculty and staff, the four Comer teams mesh together in such a way that students are wrapped in a tightly woven safety net. Consistent with Comer's focus on the "whole child," this safety net makes it difficult for students to "fall through the cracks." The Comer safety net is designed to help the school be aware of and meet the full spectrum of student needs: academic, social, medical, psychological. Some students are inclined to slip away unnoticed, but at West High, efforts are made to follow through with students in every way possible. A new teacher was amazed at West High's commitment to its student body, regardless of the children's problems:

> You know that this school is dedicated to teaching these children. They're not interested in seeing how many they can get rid of. . . . They're interested in helping these students finish high school and be the best they can be. . . . It's like no student is ever dropped off the list and forgotten.

As part of this safety net, a number of special programs have been created to support ninth-grade students, who are viewed as the most vulnerable population. West High administrators collaborate with the middle schools to begin focusing on those eighth graders with poor achievement and attendance, a combination that often leads to behavior problems in high school. The Team Success program uses a middle school model in which ninth grade students collectively take integrated core courses with the same teachers, providing enhanced opportunities for teams of teachers to identify and work collaboratively to address emerging student problems.

For West High, Comer has been a crucial mechanism for rising to meet the challenges of a difficult student population. They have used the Comer Process to develop necessary strategies and provide the supports that enable the school to be successful with this population. As the Comer facilitator for the district noted, "Comer has validated that kids we felt would never learn can learn."

Comer Contributes to a Positive Working and Learning Environment

According to a counselor, "There are no teachers bad-mouthing administration, no one is disgruntled—that's what Comer has done." At West High, Comer has provided opportunities for authentic decision making and facilitated support systems for faculty, staff, and students. Thus, it is not surprising that most faculty and staff indicated that they enjoyed working at West High and looked forward to each new school day. In spite of the hard work, long hours, and challenging students, comments such as, "I feel needed and I feel appreciated," "I feel like I'm making a difference," and "I love what I'm doing at this school," were frequently heard from faculty and support staff members. The Comer Process is credited with creating a positive environment where faculty and staff feel appreciated, valued, and professional.

A special educator admired the teachers' tireless efforts on behalf of students: "Our teachers work a lot during their planning period, during lunch, and after school with people that need additional help. That's wonderful! Over and above the call of duty, I think, but they're more than willing to do that."

The faculty's hard work and dedication did not go unnoticed by parents either, who observed, "For teachers to be here at 6:00 a.m. and then attend meetings and events after school and in the evening, I think that says a lot." Students, for the most part, believe that most teachers respect and care about them. A female student-athlete was impressed that several of her teachers took the time to drive one-and-a-half hours to show their support for the girls' basketball team.

Benchmark Goals

The most tangible evidence of the success of the Comer Process at West High is the school's attainment of its benchmark goals. The district establishes a number of "benchmarks" as determinants of each school's ongoing progress. These goals not only include student achievement on end-of-course tests, but SAT scores, the number of students taking upper level and advanced placement courses, and discipline-related issues such as attendance and suspensions. Two years ago, West High met its benchmark goals at 100%, the only high school in the system to do so. This is especially noteworthy given that West is still working to assimilate the influx of troubled students from Edison. Last year, they met their goals at 75%, which was still a respectable showing. They anticipate meeting the benchmarks at 75% again this year, which is an accomplishment considering the high numbers of at-risk students.

Although meeting the benchmark goals was a source of pride for West High faculty, staff, and students, they were not perceived as the primary indicators of the school's success. At West High the Comer Process is understood to be so pervasive that its success is not easily captured by numerical indicators. When teachers spoke of success they referred to the school's environment, student interactions, and teacher efficacy. Benchmark goals were seen as important, but they were on the periphery of their comments about what Comer means to the school.

DISSENTING VIEWS ON THE PROCESS AND AREAS FOR IMPROVEMENT

As at most schools implementing reform, there are a few dissenting teachers who do not embrace the Comer Process with enthusiasm. Although they describe the process as one that gives teachers input and uses consensus building to help teachers respect one another, they feel that the Comer Process is too time consuming, the surveys are overdone, and teachers may not really know what it means to be a Comer School.

Differential Benefits

Some teachers questioned whether the Comer Process was beneficial to all students and to high school students in particular. Do Comer principles primarily benefit the "good" students, those who would serve as leaders at any school? Does Comer continue to marginalize those students considered at-risk? At least one teacher believed that the majority of West's student body gained little from the Comer Process:

> I think the Comer Process is ill-suited for a school such as West. Consensus, no fault—with the mix of students we have, it gets lost. Only a few probably benefit from Comer. . . . The good kids get a chance, but those that aren't don't. A better mix of the student body needs to be more involved.

The real depth of Comer implementation is another critical issue. How much of the Comer Process actually filters down to the classroom level is not readily apparent. Teachers recognize the benefits that Comer team processes and principles afford, but seem reluctant to empower their students in a similar fashion. A few teachers indicated that they used Comer in their classrooms, but this was not observed in practice. Other teachers were more candid in expressing that they did not use Comer principles in the classroom because they felt a need to direct the class, to maintain control, and to be in charge of the classroom.

Furthermore, as a reform initiative designed for inner-city schools, Comer's emphasis has historically been at the elementary school level. Most of West High's student body did not attend a Comer school at either the elementary or middle school level, so their first experience with Comer was at the high school level. A few faculty members found this problematic when it came to attempting to apply the Comer principles in the classroom.

Insiders and Outsiders

Most teachers applauded the lack of cliques at West High, stating that with the Comer Process, "There was no need for cliques" and that teachers who were "not able to adjust to being the person or people in power transferred to other schools or retired." Although the majority felt there was no need for power cliques at West High since Comer implementation, this sentiment was not shared by all teachers.

Several teachers characterized the SPMT itself as an exclusive Comer inner circle, although those participating on the SPMT were not aware of their perceived elite status. These teachers were concerned that even though cliques do not exist in the school, there are teachers who are insiders in the Comer

Process and others who are outsiders. They identified insiders as the members of SPMT and IAC. Members of these teams are knowledgeable about school issues and experience decision making at different levels than other staff. Some of the others feel that although they are informed of decisions made by the teams, they remain outsiders to the process. The teachers who described themselves as outsiders acknowledged that they have input at the department level and can bring issues to SPMT and IAC members, but they still do not feel that they are inside of the decision-making loop. This teacher shared his perceptions: "There seems to be an inner Comer group where people know what's going on. I feel outside the loop, but the loop isn't closed, I just haven't pursued getting in."

Similar concerns regarding insider and outsider status were echoed in conversations with students. While many students actively participate in the Comer Process at the school governance level and cite instances in which their voices had made a difference in policies at the school, these students were aware that not all students understood the process and that participation was limited. Students who were insiders stated that the process makes students "feel great because the staff is listening to them." Others, the outsiders, recognized the use of surveys to reach consensus on some issues, but they had little knowledge of what the Comer Process was or how they could effect change in the school.

The placement of special education classes in the school also raises some concerns about how inclusive are the consensus and collaboration processes. One special education class is held in a room with entry only through the in-school suspension room. All other special education classes are held in the only trailers on the school grounds. The physical isolation of these classes seems contrary to the inclusive Comer philosophy.

Connecting Comer to the Classroom

While parents, administrators, faculty, staff, and students seemed to attribute most of the school's success to the Comer Process, questions about how much it has affected instruction still remain. West High primarily views and employs Comer as a governance process, a mechanism for site-based management. The IAC addresses curriculum issues at a general level, but otherwise it is unclear how Comer relates to the classroom. Dr. Thompson spoke eloquently about the importance of the developmental pathways as an essential component of the Comer Process:

> So many reform efforts simply deal with the academic focus, but with the Comer Process, there are six pathways critical to the learning process and we try to deal with all six as we're implementing our instructional program . . .— the physical, the social interactive, the cognitive, psycho-emotional, character development—we try to stay away from calling it moral—speech and lan-

guage, those six must be addressed as you're implementing your instructional program. If you do that successfully, then kids will be successful.

Despite this philosophical commitment, the developmental pathways are not an explicit focus of West High's Comer effort. Several faculty members could not recall any of the developmental pathways. Others believed that the developmental pathways were embedded within their curricular efforts and the School Improvement Plan. Still others saw the school's civic responsibility and character education programs as addressing Comer's ethical pathway. The current principal acknowledged that the developmental pathways have been the most difficult aspect of Comer implementation for West High. She identified the pathways as an area that needs continued work because "teachers don't always see the connections in the classroom." The challenge is applying these ideas at the high school level rather than in elementary schools where Comer has more often been implemented. Considering the developmental needs of students and focusing on the "whole child" can be foreign concepts in high schools that tend to have a fragmented structure and perspective.

No Fault: A Misunderstood Principle

West High's implementation of the Comer Process is also complicated by divergent interpretations of the no fault principle, particularly as applied to students and to discipline issues. There was agreement among teachers that with respect to their own work the no fault principle allowed them to take risks and experiment without being blamed should their efforts fail. As one teacher noted, if something does not work out as planned, "the administrators don't blame you, they sit down with you and say, 'How can we do this differently to make it successful?'" The benefit of this approach, teachers agree, is that it moves the focus away from blaming an individual to a process of evaluation, refinement, and striving for success.

As it concerned the students, however, there were sometimes contradictory interpretations of no fault. Some teachers defined no fault as everyone accepting collective responsibility for the students. Some students defined no fault as accepting responsibility for their own actions instead of assigning blame. Others, both students and faculty, believed that the no fault principle meant not blaming students for their problems but accepting them "where they are." This notion of accepting students with all of their attendant "baggage" was interpreted by other teachers as "making excuses" for students. This teacher grappled with the no fault principle as he understood it:

> I don't want to talk about no fault. I would rather be real, real firm with discipline and that doesn't seem to fit with no fault. When we start making excuses for kids—that doesn't help. Maybe we don't understand no fault the way Comer intended.

West High faculty members and support staff are sensitive to the broader socioeconomic concerns that can significantly interfere with the educational process. Teachers acknowledged that it was important to understand their students' lives beyond the school grounds. Some worried, however, that taking this understanding too far could have negative consequences due to lowered expectations in terms of personal responsibility and academic performance. They wanted to ensure that the application of no fault did not entail a total abdication of student responsibility.

Tension Between Old-Line West High and Former Edison Communities

A number of individuals indicated that in spite of the shift in student population, West has managed to retain a certain "community feeling." Yet, the school seemed to be comprised of at least two distinct communities: the old-line West High community with strong family ties and the displaced Edison students. The West students whose families have attended the school for generations fear the loss of their traditions and lament the growing lack of interest in club participation, declining attendance at sports events, and an overall decrease in school spirit over the years. The former Edison students, by contrast, expressed that their school experience has actually improved. They feel that the school has become more responsive to their needs and requests. While old-line West High students may be losing some of their traditions, the displaced Edison students are beginning to feel more like they belong.

Although the tensions among these communities are less overtly conflictual than when they were first brought together, West continues to struggle with reconciling these two distinct communities under one roof. In much the same way that Comer's processes and principles have minimized the creation of factions and cliques among the faculty members, West faculty and staff are working to create a unified West High community for students and parents. Whether or not they successfully make this transition may, in fact, impact West's future survival.

The Wrong Side of Town

West also continues to struggle with prevailing misconceptions by the larger community that it is a violent school with poor academic performance. The school's "bad reputation" is primarily a result of its location on the west side of town. These perceptions are further fueled by negative media publicity. Many members of the West High community complained that the local media does not fairly portray the school, deliberately highlighting its problems while ignoring its successes. The unfortunate result is that many students buy into the perception that they are inferior, that they do live on the wrong side of town. One of the assistant principals explained, "the self-esteem in this area [is low], they make fun of themselves being from the west side. West side trash and all this stuff."

Given the school's location, parents also recognize that they have little political power to influence school board decisions. As one parent bluntly put it, "The school board supports the east side of town because that's the part of town that supported them." Teachers indicated that West High was often ignored, as the district was "not as interested in us as they are in other schools." Ironically, most faculty members do not live in the immediate community, as one teacher who does live there explained with a laugh: "Most of us don't live here, this is the wrong side of town."

Although the school maintains a negative image within the district, outside of the county, West has been nationally recognized for many successes. Two years ago the school received a Redbook award as one of the country's most improved schools. Janice Sawyer and her predecessor, Dr. Thompson, have both received the Patrick Daly Award given annually to outstanding principals of Comer schools. West has received national recognition as a demonstration site for the Comer School Development Program. West's successes have also been recognized by the other high school principals in the school system. The former principal relates this curious phenomenon:

> But, what's interesting is that within the range of senior high school principals, West High School is perceived as being high functioning now, where great things are happening for kids. And if you go outside of [the city], 20-30 miles in any direction, then the school has an outstanding reputation.

Even today, the students, parents, teachers, and administrators describe West High as the "ugly duckling" of the metropolitan district. They feel that West is now a good school, but they are always fighting the influence of the media's ongoing perception that West High is not a successful school. The media constantly characterize the school as one besieged by violence and low productivity. Teachers stated, "we don't get the credit that we should. We have much more [positive things] going on than the public believes." As a result of the media's portrayal, the students have low self-esteem in relationship to other schools and expect that the press will use any negative event at the school to confirm their mediocrity instead of reporting on the increased achievement in recent years, their national awards, and the other positive events that occur at the school.

Because the majority of the students are from low to middle working-class families living in this western part of the city, some school personnel fear that parents and students have limited expectations and do not highly value education. Other students are viewed as rising above their difficult circumstances and succeeding in spite of the many strikes against them. A number of these students are the first in their families to graduate from high school or to seek higher education. Faculty members offer encouragement to students who might not be otherwise inclined to take advanced courses and to pursue college or some type of postsecondary education. They celebrate the success of a 21-year-old student who finally graduated and welcome the return of those students who were on the verge of dropping out of school.

An unintended consequence of West High's success with at-risk students is that the school is gaining a reputation for succeeding with challenging students who have multiple and complex problems. As this teacher observed,

> [I]t's like West High is a Statue of Liberty and we have a sign out that says, "Give me your tired, your poor, your hungry," because we take students that other schools won't take. . . . [T]hey'll come to West High and we'll take them in and try to work with them.

West must now face the reality that they will receive 70 additional at-risk students during the coming year with even fewer resources. The ever-increasing proportion of at-risk students is one of the school's greatest challenges.

CONCLUSION

West High administrators, faculty, parents, and students all credit the Comer Process for the school's survival during a time of transition and crisis. West was dealt a blow when the high school received 400 additional at-risk students who were displaced from their home school. Student safety became the paramount issue and academic achievement suffered. The school and community were ready for a change. The new principal, Dr. Thompson, initiated that change through the Comer Process. Faculty no longer felt isolated or helpless in the face of West's mounting problems. Parents no longer felt like unwelcome outsiders and students were given a voice in decision making. The faculty, staff, parents, and students were empowered to take back their school. Even a new principal did not disrupt what Dr. Thompson had set into motion.

The Comer team processes and operating principles provide mechanisms for collective action as members are now able to quickly respond to problems as they arise. These collaborative decisions also support the commonly held notion of collective responsibility for the results of those decisions as well as collective responsibility for student achievement and well-being. This emphasis on collaboration also decreases the need for factions and cliques among faculty members and has created a support system for faculty, staff, parents, and students. Consequently, West has attained benchmark goals that serve as a yardstick for increases in student achievement and decreases in discipline problems.

While the implementation of Comer at West High has resulted in a safer, more pleasant and positive place to teach and to learn, it has not been without its problems. West is still a high-maintenance school. The genuine involvement of more than just the school's "best and brightest" students in the Comer Process was raised as an issue, as was the application of Comer principles in the classroom. Although many faculty members spoke of the school's focus on the "whole child," it was not readily apparent how West was addressing Comer's six developmental pathways. Additionally, the no fault principle has been interpreted by some as a means of making excuses for students, which carries the danger of lowered expectations.

Having survived one crisis, West High is now facing new challenges as the school's population continues to shift. West is also scheduled to receive even more at-risk students as the district's attendance lines are redrawn with the opening of two new high schools. The school's ongoing battle with the media and its pervasive negative reputation within the larger community has made attracting and maintaining experienced, talented teachers even more difficult. West High seems to be approaching a new crisis in its existence that the Comer Process alone will be unable to solve. However, the school has a recent history of overcoming seemingly intractable problems and appears poised to confront these new challenges.

7

The School Development Program and School Success

George W. Noblit
University of North Carolina at Chapel Hill

As the preceding chapters demonstrate, each of the five schools has its own story, depending on its context, its unique issues, the community and students served, and the school staff who chose to implement the Comer Process. All of the schools have a host of problems to address, and before implementing Comer they responded to problems as they emerged. Although schools had some success in remedying these problems, there was no mechanism to look at all the issues and problems at once, to identify the interrelationships among issues and problems, or to develop a coordinated plan. The SDP enables staff at each of the schools to think and act more systematically. They have moved from a stance of reacting to problems to planning for success, the ultimate effect of which was to improve student performance. The SDP influences each school's success somewhat differently, but the schools share a set of themes.

The central task of this study is to explore the connections between the SDP and school success, and each of our case studies documents these connections in the particular sites. Looking at five sites as a whole allows us to reframe specifics into a set of themes that interpret how the SDP and school successes are connected. This study is limited to examining successful schools. Thus, in future studies researchers may wish to purposively select schools that vary both in the relative implementation of Comer and the relative success of the schools.

Having cases that vary on the selection criteria would help specify which factors or themes are important to the SDP's connection to school success.

Because it would be artificial to treat themes as discrete, we have tried to conceptualize them in ways that link similar practices and/or beliefs. We present these themes in an order that corresponds to our interpretation of how they build on each other and thus connect the SDP to school success. In order to understand how the SDP relates to school success, it is necessary to explore school successes, pervasive issues, taking charge of change, power and participation, valorizing professional decision making, and insuring accountability.

SCHOOL SUCCESSES

The five schools studied have a host of successes. Collectively, these schools address the challenges of being inner-city schools and their refusal to be bound to the cycle of frustration and poor achievement normally associated with inner-city schools. The staff of West High, which continues to struggle with the addition of a new population of students who are at risk of failure, refuses to accept failure as an option. They, like the staff at other schools in this study, have a sense that they are sufficiently in charge of their destiny to affect the changes needed to make these students and their school successful. Yet, it is clear that this sense is the result of a series of smaller successes that allow the school to see its destiny as different from that of its neighboring schools. In Table 7.1, we summarize the successes shared across all the schools. We discuss each of these in turn, but it is important to remember that this set derives from *successful* Comer schools. We have seen reform efforts in the United States—notably the effective schools movement-that were based on the characteristics of schools that had achieved desired ends. "Reform" schools mimicked these characteristics without understanding how successful schools made the necessary transitions and the meanings assigned to these changes. What studies of effective schools and this study share is an inability to compare the "natural histories" of schools that have reformed and those that have not. Although it seems clear to us that the SDP represents a powerful influence on the natural histories of the schools studied, it may be that these schools would have achieved what they have without the SDP or, more likely, they would have sought out or taken advantage of other reform alternatives available to them. It is entirely possible that the key variables in successful reform are having both the capacity to take advantage of reform and having the "right" reform to meet the needs of the school. There can be little doubt that Comer was "right" for these schools or that these schools had the capacity to use Comer effectively.

This said, it is clear that the SDP is a "value-added" reform. That is, it brought something to all of these schools that they did not have previously. The school community, in turn, did something with this added value. The SDP gave the schools and their communities both a new structure and a new sense of agency. As Giddens (1979) argues, structure and agency are not opposites. Each structure defines the possibilities for agency, and each act of agency, in turn, creates or recreates structure. Different structures allow different forms of agency and different forms of agency produce different structures. In each of these schools, the structures in place before the SDP were rather traditional. Traditional school structures isolate staff and students into classrooms and separate administration from instruction. The principal is then invested with the agency to act for the school as a whole. In the Comer Schools we studied, the SDP alters the traditional structure and creates opportunities for collective agency. Moreover, the schools then use this agency in the service of improving the schools. Here is where the preexisting capacity to take advantage of the reform plays out, for schools without such capacity could use collective agency to other ends, including maintaining the status quo. In short, the SDP contributed the mechanism to develop collective agency. In each of these schools, the existing capacity was not widely shared until the SDP enabled both wider participation (more shared capacity) and a way for the faculty and the community to take charge of the school's destiny.

With an expanded capacity to reform and a mechanism to take charge of reform itself, the schools we studied accomplished much. Table 7.1 summarizes these accomplishments. This exhibit shows the remarkable similarity among the schools: increased parental involvement, reduced discipline problems, improved school climate, positive transitions, and improved student achievement. Because of the recency of its adoption of Comer, Trivette Middle has not had the time to work on curricula and pedagogy or to receive external recognition. West High continues to work on building ties with the community, and continues to suffer from selective, and negative, media coverage. Merrit's accomplishments, of course, came with the first attempt with the SDP, and the new faculty unity and regenerated SDP are being used to maintain them.

The SDP, of course, instructs schools to work directly toward many of these "successes." Guided by the SDP, school staff encourage parents and the community to become involved in decision making. The SDP also focuses on changes to school climate. The focus on the developmental pathways and child-centeredness, as well as the intensive efforts of the SSST, should reduce discipline problems and help with student achievement. The comprehensive school plan, of course, is to bring all of the school's stakeholders and issues together and to organize a systemic approach to school improvement. In the case study schools, the school community uses the three mechanisms (Parent Team, SSST and SPMT); the principles of no fault, consensus, and collaboration; the representative governance system; and the comprehensive school plan to focus on the needs of the children, using the developmental pathways to consider what is in the children's best interest. The school communities, in turn, decided to work on curriculum and instruction, positive transitions, external recognition, achievement, and discipline. Furthermore, the schools have leveraged their successes to

Table 7.1. Comer School Successes.

	Oceanview Elementary School	Gregory Elementary School	Merrit Elementary School	Trivette Elementary School	West Elementary School
With parents	•increased parental involvement and confidence in the school	•increased parental involvement and confidence in the school	•increased parental involvement and confidence in the school	•increased parental involvement and confidence in the school	•increased parental involvement and confidence in the school
In the community	•unified a multiethnic community behind the school •improved the image of the school within the community	•unified two communities behind the school •improved the image of the school within the community	•created strong ties with the community •improved the image of the school within the community	•improved the image of the school within the community	
With discipline	•reduced discipline problems	•reduced discipline problems	•reduced discipline problems	•reduced discipline problems	•reduced discipline problems
Within the school climate	•improved teacher satisfaction and sense of efficacy •created a sense of community and shared purpose •created a positive working and learning environment	•improved teacher satisfaction and sense of efficacy •created a sense of community and shared purpose •overcame racial divisiveness; desegregated within	•increased teacher and student self-esteem and morale •increased school pride •created a safe haven for students and staff	•improved teacher satisfaction and sense of efficacy •created a sense of community and shared purpose •created a positive working and learning environment	•improved teacher satisfaction and sense of efficacy •created a sense of community and shared purpose •created a positive working and learning environment

Table 7.1. Comer School Successes (con't).

		the school	•recreated faculty unity	•exploring Paideia with the SDP	•created an instructional team
	•created a safe haven for students and staff				
Within curriculum and pedagogy	•incorporated developmental pathways into instruction	•created a coherent and aligned curriculum			
With positive transitions	•embraced downsizing as "good for the students" •embraced changing teaching staff to meet the needs of shifting student population	•acquired new school building	•"saved" the school from being closed •regenerating the SDP	•improving reputation	•helped school survive the addition of a large number of students •survived a principal change
With external recognition	•received several grants and awards	•received several grants and awards	•received several awards		•received several national awards
On achievement tests	•increased student achievement	•increased student achievement	•increased student achievement •performed well in district and area competitions	•increased minority achievement scores	•increased student achievement scores

get additional resources, grants, and personnel. They have learned how to use success to their own ends; they use the Comer Process to create their *own* programs for reform.

The SDP, obviously, is a powerful structure for these schools. Yet we would underscore a major tenet of the SDP: It is what the schools *do* with the SDP that leads to these successes. These schools used the agency fostered by the SDP to promote inclusiveness, improvement, and ultimately reform. They have changed the trajectory that their previous histories projected. Instead of being mired in and demoralized by the many problems facing urban schools, they used the SDP to create a new future for themselves. The result is that these schools not only have achieving students, they become attractive places. Community members want their children to go to these schools, to the point that some parents try to get their children enrolled even though they live out of the district the school serves.

PERVASIVE ISSUES

Although the list of successes shared by these schools is impressive, it is ironic that all of the schools also viewed these same issues as ongoing concerns (see Table 7.2). These schools continue to work on parent and community involvement, cross-cultural communication, and improving instruction and student achievement. The SDP has enabled the schools to address these issues, but issues are likely to persist. In addition, the schools nominated issues that they have not had time to address fully. This is especially the case with curriculum reform at Trivette Middle. Merrit's remaining issues reflect the difficulty it has had with ingroup-outgroup dynamics. West High continues to struggle with its public image. Taken together, the issues represent persistent problems of urban education and educational reform that are less amenable to permanent resolution. These problems are "facts of life" that urban schools must accommodate everyday. They also testify to the fragility of school improvement. The similarities across all the schools are graphic evidence that accomplishments must always be recreated and improved. This point cannot be overemphasized. These schools have to be forever vigilant to maintain their status, and even so they cannot escape vulnerability to changes in district leadership or state policy.

TAKING CHARGE OF CHANGE

Each of the school stories reveals that one of the most powerful contributions of the SDP to the schools' successes is a new orientation to change. Many educational reforms work both to specify what changes should happen in the school

Table 7.2. Pervasive Issues.

	Oceanview Elementary School	Gregory Elementary School	Merrit Elementary School	Trivette Elementary School	West Elementary School
With parents	•parent-school communication and translations	•parent involvement	•parent involvement	•parent involvement	•parent involvement
With the community	•community ties	•community ties	•community ties	•community ties	•community ties •negative public image •lack of constituent "clout" with the school board
Within the school	•cross-cultural communication and understanding •overcrowding	•cross-cultural communication and understanding	•cross-cultural communication and understanding •integration of bilingual program and staff into the larger context of the school		•cross-cultural communication and understanding •faculty turnover
With the physical space	•space		•space		•fair and adequate space for all departments
With instruction	•cross-program instruction	•instruction	•altering instruction	•instruction •altering instruction	•instruction
With students	•student achievement	•student achievement	•student achievement	•student achievement	•student achievement

and to limit change to the specific reform. Indeed, reforms that are "packaged" so that they can be implemented without alteration may promote improved achievement, but those reforms also limit the capacity of the school to understand when change is necessary, to be able to critically evaluate different reforms, and to understand how to change. "Packaged" reforms leave the school as vulnerable to changes in the community, students, and district and state educational policies as they were before they chose the "package." The SDP is more a process than a "package"—one that helps the school to take charge of change.

Oceanview Elementary is the richest example of contextual change. The Comer Process has enabled Oceanview to learn about change, to work through the issues, and to use the SDP to organize change. Oceanview has used the Comer Process to, in fact, reconstruct itself in order to better serve the children. This is a powerful demonstration of taking charge of change, but the other schools are using the SDP in similar ways: Merritt changed the school climate; West High added an instructional council; and Trivette Middle enabled teachers to implement changes that had been suppressed.

The SDP has enabled the staff at Gregory School to take charge of the mandated local school council. The SDP helps those within the school and community to develop a school plan that has widespread support. Previous to Comer the local school councils were formed to provide a closer link to the community. It is ironic that the SDP is, in fact, more broadly participatory and therefore has proved more successful in providing that community link. Gregory School responds to the needs of a wide community, rather than to the opinions of a few community representatives. This is another powerful example of how the SDP enables the case study schools to take charge of change instead of being subject to changes beyond their control.

Taking charge of change, of course, is a complex endeavor. These schools suggest that it requires: (a) a preexisting base for the SDP, (b) instituting cultural change, and (c) actually making changes happen.

A Base for Reform

As noted previously, each of these schools had a base on which the SDP could build. In all the schools, a strong and relatively new principal is a key aspect of this base. Yet, it appears that a strong principal alone is insufficient as a base for reform. At Trivette Middle, teachers were ready for change and had begun to work together on instructional improvements. Furthermore, Trivette's district was advocating Comer as a reform. At Oceanview and Gregory, the community was anxious for change. Merritt and Gregory both had successfully resolved threats to the schools' existence and pulled together the staffs and communities. Thus, their base included the principal, staff and community unity and a sense of political capacity.

Coupled with the base in each of these schools is a sense of need. Trivette Middle teachers felt a need to address what was happening in their school. Oceanview's need derived from a change in student populations. West High's need came from poor leadership and a change in student population, Merrit and Gregory had crises about the survival of the school. Finally, as we will discuss later, all the schools were facing an external demand for improvements in student achievement. The SDP helps transform locally and externally defined needs into goals to be pursued. The strong principals who were new to each of the schools are central in shaping the need, fostering the belief that "something must be done," and pressing a sense of urgency into the search for what must be done. This, in turn, allows the SDP to be considered and ultimately chosen. With a base for reform and a sense of need, the SDP becomes an enabling mechanism.

Cultural Change

The schools we studied are best understood as existing in a milieu in which change is ubiquitous. The students they serve are changing. The districts in which they are embedded are in flux and demanding that schools change. Prior to the arrival of new principals and the SDP, the prevalent belief among staff and community members was that little could be done, but this belief has now changed. With the SDP, the teachers are gaining a sense of control over their own destinies. That is, the SDP is the vehicle for cultural change in these schools. It is remarkable to us that even though the SDP represents a change in itself, it works to manage change, giving the school and its community a belief that they can control their school's destiny. Prior to Comer, the staffs at the schools said the context of change was unsettling, threatening, and something to be avoided if possible. With Comer, these same people now manage change.

Environmental changes are, in many ways, facts of life in urban schools and, although the individual schools are not able to arrest environmental changes, the SDP does allow the schools and communities to control what they can and shape what they cannot control. Through SDP, they generate solidarity in the face of repeated challenges to their ability to control their destinies. For example, Gregory Elementary School exists within the context of the numerous reform movements the district has undertaken. Physical change was manifest in the building of the new school. Social change was apparent in the school's attempt to foster a sense of community by encouraging interaction and understanding between Chinese and black students. Similarly, shifting demographics and adapting to change have been the most prevalent issues confronting Merrit Elementary in recent years. The school is changing from an almost entirely African American school and neighborhood to one that is more multicultural and bilingual. For Oceanview Elementary School, change has become an accepted part of the school culture as the demographics of the school population and the surrounding neighborhood shift. High mobility of students as well as cultural groups are no longer problems. They have provided focus for the school, and in doing so revitalized the linkages between the school and community. Trivette Middle has changed its reputation for the better. West High's population has recovered from an abrupt change in its demographics so that many African American students feel that the school has become more responsive to their needs. The SDP provides all these schools with an ideological framework to accept change and to adapt to shifting populations. Having a sense of control over one's destiny is a significant cultural accomplishment for each of these schools. The next step-moving from having a sense of control to actually taking charge of change-involves making changes.

Making Changes

The Comer Process allows schools to effect change. In schools we studied the SDP has undermined the control of dominant groups of faculty, students, or parents by inviting wide participation. The principles of no fault, collaboration and consensus have proved to be key resources for creating change. School principals and teachers repeatedly cite the institution of the no fault principle as an important change in itself for the schools. Assigning blame blocks the design of remedies, focuses the schools' attention on failures rather than on potential solutions, and splits schools into factions. Instituting a process that emphasizes collaboration and consensus altered how decisions were made and contributed to the elimination of factions among the faculty in all but one school.

Similarly, the SDP has been a vehicle for all the schools to address curricular issues, to create or realign bilingual programs, to align curricula and testing, and to develop new instructional programs. Staff in at least four of the schools used the three Comer principles to address ethnic separations, enabling a transition to a more multicultural school. This is an extremely heartening development for these schools and should serve as inspiration for all schools that are struggling with changing communities and more diverse student bodies. The SDP provides a mechanism to insure multicultural representation in schools, making multiculturalism a resource for change rather than a problem.

Making changes and seeing resultant positive effects helped the schools we studied believe in taking charge of change. The SDP also encourages school communities to take charge of change through power and participation, valorizing professional decision making, and insuring accountability.

POWER AND PARTICIPATION

Reform, urban education, and race are all entangled with power. Indeed, that state and district reforms have focused on urban minority schools testifies to the relative lack of power these schools and people have in education. As discussed earlier, however, the SDP summons power to the schools which then allows them to challenge the historic equation that urban schools equal peoples of color and powerlessness. The SDP is in many ways a governance system, defining the rules of participation through the mechanisms of the Parent Team, the SSST and the SPMT, and the principles of no fault, collaboration and consensus, designating who gets to participate, and requiring a focus on children.

Yet, for several reasons, participation is not equal in practice. First, in most schools, students are not active in the Comer Process, which is true even in the one school that has a student SPMT. Even though SDP training argues for using the SDP in the classroom, teachers have not considered the SDP as a model for classroom governance. They have not yet considered that classrooms would be a natural extension of the SDP. We are left with the concern that, as important as the SDP is to these schools, participants have not seen the experience with the SDP as having implications beyond its current usage. This suggests that school staff are not thinking about the natural extension of the SDP to other arenas of the school organization. This is a severe limitation in the staffs' understanding of change itself. We feel the benefits these schools ascribe to the SDP are too significant to be reserved for adults. Second, it is also true that in practice, teachers participate more than parents. This seems inevitable in a reform that focuses on what schools can do for children. Parents may be so grateful for the increased participation afforded by the SDP that they are not concerned about teacher power in the process. Moreover, as Delpit (1995) argues, among a number of cultural groups, the expectation is for the teacher to be authoritative. The SDP does not prescribe any group's dominance of the process. Thus, the dominance of teachers may not be an important issue. As the schools continue to emphasize parent involvement, the salience of increased power to increased involvement may be better discerned. Nonetheless, parents also have increased their power. Furthermore, it is clear to us that parent involvement in these schools is much more than simply assuring the representation of parent interests. The SDP training for parents helps prepare them for successful political participation both in the SDP and in the wider community. In these schools, the principals and staffs mobilize parents to serve as political forces in the service of the school and the children. Teachers may have more power than parents in the SDP decision-making process. Parents experience their power in community and school district struggles.

To fully understand power and participation, however, it is necessary to sort out the school district involvement, the special nature of principal power, and the salience of teacher power in these schools.

School District Involvement

In the real world of school reform, the involvement of the school district in promoting reform is a double-edged sword. If the district chooses a reform it often happens that some schools will interpret that reform as being imposed and may generate opposition to the reform and/or district officials. On the other hand, if a district allows schools to choose reforms on their own and tries to avoid favoritism by supporting each chosen reform equitably, it is vulnerable to accusations that it lacks commitment to any particular reform. The SDP is a case in point. Some district-wide Comer initiatives have been shown to have positive effects on student performance (Comer & Haynes, 1992) but lost their momentum with a change of superintendents. This leads to the conclusion that the reform was the superintendent's agenda and not the schools' agenda. On the other hand, Neufeld and LaBue (1994) argue that the difficulties Comer schools faced in Hartford were in part due to the fact that the district had sponsored a number of school-level initiatives and evidenced a lack of commitment to the Comer Process per se. Yet, in both of these cases, it appears to us that an alternative explanation is that the schools themselves did not assume the responsibility for the reform.

District involvement was a small part of the story in our case study schools. For the most part, the school districts provided funds for training, Comer facilitators (often shared across schools), and other incidental expenses. Yet, only one of the five schools, Trivette, had a significant district-level initiative. For Trivette Middle School, three things mitigated the risk of the SDP being perceived as imposed. First, the SDP came in with a new principal who was a favorite of the superintendent. Second, the teachers perceived the principal's arrival as an indication that the school was once again in the district's favor. Third, the Comer Process itself is so focused on local site decision-making that it undercut any notion that implementing the process primarily served the superintendent's interests and political ambitions.

On the other hand, the case of Gregory Elementary demonstrates school-level responsibility for the SDP in the strong connection between the local school council (LSC) and the Comer Process. Although administration of the Comer Process occurs through an independent educational agency, the decision to implement the SDP at Gregory was still a function of the LSC. Therefore, the implementation and the administration of the SDP effectively avoided any notion that its primary purpose was to serve the interests and political ambitions of the superintendent. The SDP was a school and community commitment.

As we will discuss later, a sense of accountability to the community is vital in these schools. The lesson seems to be that in addition to funding training, facilitators, and incidental expenses, districts should consider how to build a base for reform in the school, and a localized perception of the need for

Comer (or any reform) so that it makes sense to the school and its community. In these schools, selecting a new principal for the school was the important decision. These principals were a key part of the base and promoted the need for reform.

Principal Power

The power of the principal is critical to SDP implementation. Unlike the principals in Neufeld and LaBue's (1994) study, in which the principals were unsure of their authority, the principals of these Comer schools are dynamic leaders who understand power and are not afraid to use it. Each principal championed Comer, albeit in somewhat different ways. In West High, the principal began to implement the SDP before it was even named. In Trivette, the new principal brought Comer with him. In the other schools, a relatively new principal proposed and negotiated Comer.

Moreover, in important respects, the SDP actually serves as a check and balance for the principal's power. For example, the West High principal who initiated Comer used his power to provide teachers and staff with professional development in the Comer Process, to entice staff to read books about Comer, and to convince staff that he could, in fact, make changes in the school by finding a place for a teachers' lounge. The principal at Merrit summarized well 13 leadership strategies that seemed to characterize all the principals. He offered that Comer principals need to:

1. Initially institute a structure and an attitude of mutual respect;
2. Try out new ideas and see if they work;
3. Make the school a center of community advocacy;
4. Expose the students to the wider world both to discover opportunities and demonstrate their capabilities to themselves;
5. Recognize classroom successes based on results rather than on a shared philosophy;
6. Use challenges to build senses of unity and efficacy;
7. Ask people to reflect on and consider changes;
8. Insure the SDP is representative in fact and not just in structure;
9. Share the SDP training, leadership, and power to keep a broad base of participation;
10. Approach the SDP creatively;
11. Focus the SDP on curriculum and instruction;
12. Let the SPMT make the decisions that stakeholders will actually implement; and
13. Insure the SDP is faithfully enacted.

This list of leadership strategies is remarkable in that it defines the principal's role not as a decision maker or as the final authority. Rather the principal is to lead by: initiating a set of activities, concentrating on cultural changes, and enforcing the SDP.

The principal at Oceanview Elementary School is a strong believer in Comer and her leadership models the Comer Process. Staff and district personnel say that "She doesn't just talk the talk, but walks the walk." Mrs. Knight at Gregory School earned and secured her position through a masterful use of power both within and outside the school. She then ushered in the SDP as a means for increasing student achievement and facilitating parent involvement, but in the end she believes Comer was responsible for her evolution as a leader. In each of these schools, the formation of the SDP Teams created a new decision-making system that empowered parents and teachers and balanced the power of the principal. Each of these dynamic principals would be perceived as overbearing without the SDP to balance his or her power. Indeed, the principal at Gregory School speaks for these principals when she says, "the Comer Process taught me how to lead."

The checking and balancing of the principal's power seems to work on at least two levels. First, to the teachers in these schools, "being heard" is important to their commitment to the school. In fact, "being heard" can sometimes provide sufficient impetus for teachers to rally behind proposals from the principal or other teachers they had initially questioned. Second, the principles of collaboration and consensus set norms for decision making that push the principals to negotiate if they wish to influence a decision. This changes how principals usually work (Noblit & Johnston, 1982). The no fault principle also reduces the threat of principal sanction in the decision-making process. Finally, as a formal structure, the SPMT distributes responsibility for decisions and implementation of those decisions. To use Comer's phrase, "school power" is increased even if the principal has to adjust his or her style of leadership to work effectively in a more participatory, consensual process. This process has most fully evolved at West High, where a dynamic principal began the SDP but was succeeded by a principal who "trusts the process" of shared decision making.

The SDP is least developed at Merrit Elementary, where the principal directs the process. On the one hand, this principal uses the Comer ideology of child-centered decision making as a justification for decisions that legitimize his power. On the other hand, the Comer Process sometimes serves to check his power as teacher teams collaborate and make decisions. In the other schools, the SDP has given the community and staff more power and has permitted the principal to be powerful in implementing decisions, representing the school, and identifying issues and defining their urgency. The staffs at these schools indicate that having a strong leader contributed to their ability to affect the destiny of their schools. As noted earlier, although the SDP seems to increase the power of parents considerably, the teachers more directly benefited. As one member of our team noted, the SDP "assumes school is good for you" and, as a result, decisions serve the interests of the teachers. To be fair, the parents and community members we interviewed share this assumption and thus do not see the stratification of power in favor of the teachers as a problem. Parents have come to trust that the teachers will act in the best interests of the children. Of course, balancing power in the school ultimately benefits the students, even if they are not direct participants in the process.

Teacher Power

The SDP has a remarkable effect on the micropolitics of the school, especially those involving the teachers. Four of these schools report that there are no cliques or factions among the teachers. Clearly, there are friendship groups, lunch groups, and curriculum teams, as well as other groups, but in our experience a school without cliques or factions is rare. We have concluded that the SDP has not eliminated micropolitics in these schools; rather, it effectively aligns the informal power structure with the formal. Put this way, the SPMT is the elite ingroup. Because the SPMT is consciously representative of various constituencies, it has not been seen to be as "political" as teacher cliques or groups prior to the implementation of SDP. The atmosphere of collaboration and consensus engendered by the SDP has pushed the interests of the teachers to the forefront of the school community. Furthermore, early political successes have contributed to the absence of factions among the faculty. At West High a vocational teacher summarized the group feeling when she said, "Everyone was willing to give up their individual wants and needs for the good of the school. We wear a team badge!" West High teachers and the teachers from Gregory, Oceanview, and Trivette benefit from the Comer Process because they share curriculum material, have a unified focus, work on interdisciplinary projects, and plan interventions for troubled students. This sharing was incidental and unusual prior to the Comer Process.

In many schools, teachers feel isolated from one another as well as from parents and administrators. The SDP brings these groups together and allows teachers a chance to voice concerns to parents and administrators in a forum that emphasizes the values and norms of the school culture. Yet, there is also a second and important reason for unity in these schools. Bringing in the SDP was also a way to encourage staff who were dissatisfied to leave and then to hire new staff who were willing to commit to the SDP and to the principal. In this way, new and veteran faculty shared a commitment. At West High, teachers consistently applauded the lack of cliques. They stated that with the Comer Process, "There was no need for cliques." Teachers who were "not able to adjust to being the person or people in power transferred to other schools or retired." Yet, West High also demonstrates that ingroup-outgroup sentiments are always lingering in schools. Several teachers alluded to the impression that the SPMT itself serves as the Comer inner circle, but those participating on the

SPMT were not aware of their perceived elite status. These teachers were concerned that even though cliques did not exist in the school, there were teachers who were insiders and others who were outsiders. They identified insiders as the members of SPMT and the Instructional Advisory Committee (IAC). The teachers who described themselves as outsiders acknowledged that they have input at the department levels and can bring issues to SPMT and IAC members, but they still do not feel that they are inside the decision-making loop. One teacher shared his perceptions: "There seems to be an inner Comer group where people know what's going on. I feel outside the loop, but the loop isn't closed, I just haven't pursued getting in." Whereas West High demonstrates the potential for cliques in even these schools, Merrit School is an example of how they affect the SDP when they emerge, generating political factions and undercutting the school's progress. As a result, the principal has taken responsibility for regenerating faculty unity and the SDP.

VALORIZING PROFESSIONAL DECISION MAKING

Urban schools are increasingly unable to find certified and capable teachers. Teacher education programs across the country do not attract students to fill the teaching vacancies in most urban schools. Districts are relying on people with little or no training in education such as long-term substitutes, participants of alternative training programs like Teach for America, and graduates of lateral entry or mid-career teacher programs to fill their faculties. This situation is exacerbated by inadequate materials, less-than-desirable educational environments for learning, and the pressure of high-stakes assessment programs. Furthermore, schools are often overcrowded, have many students who are disruptive, and do not have the necessary equipment for science and other technical instruction. In many urban school settings the extant philosophy is more one of "getting through the day" than of reforming education.

As a result, many teachers lecture or "teach by telling." The teacher's goal is to tell students the proper procedures to perform and then to give them an opportunity to practice executing the procedures. Teaching by telling also intensifies the focus on teaching as knowledge transfer, makes students passive learners, and simplifies the demands of planning and classroom management (Smith, 1996). Most importantly, this teaching does not address the diverse needs of students in the schools and does not help many students to be successful.

This is the instructional context that the Comer Process inherits when it moves into urban schools. Even though the SDP has little specified educational context, Comer's proposals exudes faith that people of color and teachers in urban schools can make education work for poor children. This faith was well-rewarded in the case study schools. Each school used the SDP to align curricula and promote student achievement.

Although our observations of classrooms in the Comer schools revealed that instruction was not generally different from the instruction in other schools—some instruction was exemplary and some marginal—Comer provided teachers with the instructional advantage of having a general focus and a direction that enabled them to work collectively toward the common goal of student achievement. Generally, the Comer model has been implemented in schools in which the prior focus was on teaching students to obey the rules. Those who obeyed the rules were rewarded with more academic programs and more interesting instruction. Those who did not obey the rules were destined to lower tracks, special programs for at-risk students, and exceptional education. With the inception of the Comer model, the educational emphasis was transformed from obedience to enlightenment. The guiding principles of consensus, no fault, and collaboration provided the foundation for teachers and administrators to think more about what was good for children rather than what was good for the schools and teachers. The School Development Program, by emphasizing home-school connections, responding to students with difficulties, and using the developmental pathways to identify and plan for the needs of children, encourages educators to think about ways to include students in the educational process rather than to exclude them if they do not respond to traditional methods of instruction. Thus, the educators are asked to think about what needs to be done to enlighten children rather than think of ways to have them conform to the system.

In the case study schools, the Comer Process creates the opportunities for educators to begin conversations about the instruction and education of their students, especially those students who present educational challenges. The Comer schools in this study actively use the guiding principles to reduce the salience of the factors limiting inner-city teaching and to consider how to focus on enlightenment in their schools. Because many policymakers and educators consider high schools to be the most difficult to reform, we use West High as a prime example of how the SDP can be used to address instruction. West High teachers felt the need for an instructional component that had parallel authority to the other Comer teams. They created the Instructional Advisory Committee (IAC), consisting of department chairs, administrators, and other support staff. They also established numerous teacher committees to support instructional reform. Aware that the SSMT (their version of the SSST) would handle individual student problems, they felt that the IAC would allow them to take an holistic approach to the education of *all* students in their school. West High uses the Comer model to address the needs of all of the students in the school. They track student achievement at their school through state-mandated, end-of-course testing. The IAC and teacher committees use the data generated by the testing to determine weaknesses in the educational programs. They use this data to align and strengthen weak instructional programs to be consistent with recommended models for achievement. They plan the necessary professional development for teachers to support teacher change in content knowledge and pedagogy. The focused interaction encouraged among content-area teachers in department meetings and the interdisciplinary committees feed into the development of school-wide plans for improved achievement. They use the developmental pathways as the theoretical underpinnings of academic and ethical programs that address civic responsibility, character education, and personal development. The teachers at West High used and continue to use the SDP to improve their instructional program, even when many reformers doubt the ability of teachers to do this.

The other schools demonstrate similar processes. At Trivette, the Comer Process is the umbrella structure for making decisions about instructional programs; these decisions have led to increased achievement. The school is now exploring an instructional reform, Paideia, as a way to continue to improve. Oceanview uses the SDP to help make better decisions about how to appropriately serve their multilingual-multicultural students. Gregory focuses on the state accountability system, aligning its curricula with the testing program to much improved results. It also uses the SDP to consider and add enrichment programs to overcome the narrow definitions of success in the state accountability system.

The SDP only asks the schools to focus on the needs of the students, and leaves the design of the instructional program up to those who are closest to the children—the parents, educators, and community members. Although there is reason to be concerned about the quality of teachers in urban areas, the case study schools had sufficient capability to design improved instructional programs. Part of this is likely to be the result of the teacher turnover each school experienced with the introduction of Comer. Teachers left, and were encouraged to leave, if they were not willing to buy into the SDP. New teachers were hired based on their commitment to the SDP and their teaching abilities. In short, the implementation of the SDP meant that the faculties at these schools were no longer those of the typical inner-city school.

Allowing teachers the freedom to organize their own curriculum gave credence to the professional decision-making capabilities of the teaching staff. Additionally, the atmosphere of consensus and collaboration allowed the teachers a voice in the education process—a voice that the previous power dynamics and bureaucracy had stifled. Indeed, the SDP gives new permission to express and act on one's beliefs about how best to teach. In the case study schools, the SDP does even more. It valorizes professional decision making by teachers. It assumes teachers know best and allows individual teachers to teach as they think best.

Yet, although consensus is a principle of SDP decision making, no consensus exists in any of these schools about how the teachers should teach. It should be said that this is not unusual in education. Whereas curricular content has been aligned with state and district standards and tests, states, districts, and principals all have left instruction largely up to individual teachers. In part, this is because requiring a uniform mode of instruction creates factions in the teaching force, undercutting the reform itself (see Muncey & McQuillan, 1996).

Recent efforts to link the SDP with a particular instructional program may be a direct test of this proposition. Trivette Middle is now attempting to implement the Paideia Program as part of a district effort, and teachers will be asked to change their practice. To our way of thinking, it is not a question of whether Paideia or other curricular-instructional reform is effective with students. If an instructional reform is viewed by teachers as imposed, the effect is the opposite of valorizing professional decision making. This may lead to teacher resistance, which may then spill over into SDP. Many reforms are based on distrust of teacher professional decision making, and proponents of such reforms point to Merrit School as a case demonstrating Comer's faith in teachers is misplaced. Last year, there was no consensus about pedagogy. Teachers were free to engage in any instructional practice provided that the students achieved at high levels. Unfortunately, these practices included ability grouping and tracking, an exclusive focus on phonics, or highly structured classrooms that emphasized control. Yet this year, Merrit is also reestablishing faculty unity, which may lead to a new understanding of what is good practice. West High also has some ingroup-outgroup dynamics. Yet, when power is balanced and the faculty is unified, valorizing professionalization decision making by teachers has led to curricular and instructional reforms and changes in student achievement, attendance, and discipline. We would need case studies of a range of Comer schools to examine these patterns and more fully address whether teachers can be "trusted" to make good decisions about pedagogy.

We would also note that our research team did not observe reflective conversations between teachers. This may be simply data we missed, but it would seem that a systemic reflection on teaching would allow teachers to consider their own belief systems about teaching and learning while at the same time reflecting and contemplating about how their own students learn. This does not force a consensus on the "one best way" to teach, but rather lets each teacher improve her or his own approach to instruction.

INSURING ACCOUNTABILITY

The recent reform era has led to the development of state and district policies that are designed to increase accountability of schools and teachers. Accountability policy has shifted the primary intent of educational policy from controlling the process of schooling to controlling outcomes. This change has dramatic implications for all schools, but accountability policy has especially strong implications for urban, minority schools such as the five we studied; accountability policy is race and poverty blind in ways educational policy has never been. The assumption is that being held accountable will *force* schools to "make" poor and minority children achieve in ways we have rarely seen in the public schools. The case study schools have used the SDP to address accountability policies and have had some successes. The case study of Gregory School well reflects these issues. Gregory School has streamlined its curriculum and instructional program to fit the state testing and high stakes accountability system. Its success at this means district officials regard Gregory as an "exemplary" school. Yet this must be taken in context. Gregory School is not achieving like suburban schools. It is exemplary in the achievement gains, not in the level of achievement. Gregory School exemplifies the tradeoff inherent in accountability policy. To successfully address high-stakes testing programs, they have reduced the curriculum-this tradeoff is well known in the research literature (Corbett & Wilson, 1991; Darling-Hammond, & Wise, 1985).

It is important to understand that these and other urban schools are unlikely to "will" the achievement of their minority students, even with dramatic changes in curricula and instructional programs. It is not that these students, or schools, or communities are incapable. Our case studies suggest the opposite. Capability is a hallmark of these schools and the SDP has much to do with this. Instead, the issue is that accountability policy is itself racist. Claude Steele's research shows that "high-stakes" testing (Corbett & Wilson, 1991) produces a pattern of test results that understate the accomplishments of African American students. Steele's research (1993, 1995, 1997) shows again and again that racial vulnerability leads to a disidentification with achievement, and this is represented in standardized test results. Steele's research also shows that high-stakes testing insures not achievement, but systematic differences in test results between minorities and middle-class whites (Steele, 1993, 1995, 1997). It is also important to note that even though Steele (1992) cites Comer's work in New Haven as an example of how to overcome racial vulnerability and disidentification, accountability policy has now changed the context for the SDP. Narrow definitions of school success lead to a narrow curriculum and heighten the effects of racial vulnerability on test results. The case study schools can point to successes but, Steele's research suggests it is unlikely that these schools will demonstrate they can achieve at levels equal to suburban schools. High-stakes testing may well insure a test score ceiling for the achievement outcomes from the SDP or any other reform of urban schools.

Internal Accountability

Whereas high-stakes testing programs enforce an external definition of accountability, the SDP is about internal accountability in schools. In each of the case study schools, the focus was on what was good for the students. The SDP facilitated effective decision making through its mechanisms (Parent Team, SSST, SPMT) and its principles (no fault, consensus, and collaboration) as well as by embedding the decisions in a process of child-centered planning. Furthermore, the developmental pathways remind the schools to consider the children holistically, helping to counter the narrowed definitions of external accountability policy.

In each of these schools, a sense of need was part of the decision to adopt the Comer Process. These needs were broadly defined and included issues of reducing racial and ethnic segregation within the school, improving order in the school, and involving parents and community, as well as academic achievement. The planning process and the inclusiveness of the SDP's governance system has generated, in the case study schools, a strong sense of internal accountability. These schools are responsible to their communities for all the needs they identify. Recall that the schools also regarded many of their successes as pervasive issues for them. Instead of deciding that the problems with the schools had been solved, and the schools could turn their attention to other issues, these successful Comer schools continue to see themselves as accountable for their problems and continue to work on them.

The sense of internal accountability in these schools has also worked to counter the narrow external accountability criteria. More importantly, the schools' strong sense of internal accountability means that what is being *externally* defined as important is one of the things for which the schools are *internally* accountable. The case study schools know that being successful on external standards contributes to the sense of efficacy and is important to the future success of the students. Student's educational opportunities are determined by their individual performances on standardized tests.

A sense of local accountability is also important in keeping the parents and community involved. When the school is serving the needs of the community and parents, the parents and community reciprocate by supporting the school. In turn, these schools mobilized the parents and community when thee were political struggles. Internal accountability is transformed into political prowess in each of these schools.

SUMMARY

The stories of the five successful Comer schools are each unique. In comparing them, however, it becomes apparent there are a set of themes significant in all the schools. These themes, in turn, allow a more nuanced understanding of how the School Development Program is connected to the successes these schools have had. The SDP helped the schools "take charge" of change. It also aligned informal and formal power in the schools taking advantage of district support; redefining the power of the principal, teachers, and parents; and creating a more participatory governance process. In these schools, the Comer Process involved valorizing the professional decision making of teachers, which led to new instructional programs and improved student achievement. The SDP also helped to promote a strong sense of internal accountability for the students, which in turn has helped the schools be more accountable to external standards.

These themes, of course, are not independent. In real life, they feed on each other, creating more than the sum of the themes themselves. In the next chapter, we represent how this synergy works in the case study schools.

8

The School Development Program and Education Reform

George W. Noblit
University of North Carolina at Chapel Hill

Jean A. Patterson
Wichita State University

For many reasons the School Development Program looms large in the stories of these five schools. First, the SDP is the reform they have chosen to help them improve their schools. Second, it has become their primary decision-making and governance mechanism. Third, it has expanded the definition of "participant in the school" to include community members, parents, students, staff, and faculty. Fourth, the SDP facilitated a number of accomplishments, breeding both a sense of control over the schools' destinies and a sense of efficacy that spurs people to further efforts to improve. Finally, the SDP empowers people with the realization that it is they who make the difference. The SDP provides the mechanism for them to do what is needed and important. The people in these schools and communities have learned to value a governance process that is the vehicle for so much good. They refer to the Comer Process as the change that has made the difference in their schools.

These five schools were in many ways ripe for change, but not just any reform would have accomplished what Comer did. Reforms that prescribe an instructional approach may well change classroom practice and increase test scores, but they are less likely to provide a mechanism for systemic change within the school and between the school and community. These schools used the SDP to alter their curricula and instructional programs and for many other things, including:

1. Taking charge of change;
2. Building on existing assets and strengths;
3. Communicating across the many stakeholder groups;
4. Framing and pursuing concerns, issues, and needs;
5. Developing power for the parents and community, and redesigning the power of the principal;
6. Insuring internal accountability;
7. Valorizing professional decision making;
8. Addressing issues of race; and
9. Restructuring and reculturing these schools.

Taken together these themes created a sense of efficacy in these case study schools. This sense of efficacy was a significant factor that resulted in structural and cultural change. If they had chosen a reform that was primarily about curriculum and/or instruction, these schools would have focused their efforts on classrooms and kept their existing governance system. There is little reason to believe they would have developed the generalized senses of control and efficacy that they now have. To improve achievement, a school does need to focus on students, curricula, and instruction, but to improve a school it is necessary to change its structure *and* culture.

As these case studies illustrate, school reform is a complex, often elusive process not easily captured as a framework, prescription, or blueprint for change. Although each of these schools achieved similar outcomes using the same reform process, each school's story and context is very different. Each school adapted the structure of the SDP while remaining true to Comer's underlying philosophy that emphasized creating structures that support students, faculty, and parents.

Tacit Assumptions about Schooling

Astuto, Clark, Read, McGree, and Fernandez (1994) argue that school reform efforts typically fail to recognize, much less examine, the tacit assumptions that are held about the purpose of education, about people in schools, and about how schools should be organized. These normative assumptions are so deeply embedded and mutually reinforcing that it becomes difficult to disentangle them and hold them up for scrutiny. Tacit assumptions also inhibit our ability to think about alternatives for what is possible in schools as they provide the standard against which our beliefs about education are measured. Thus, in order to achieve systemic change for schools, these taken-for-granted assumptions must be revealed and examined.

Much of the extant school reform literature that calls for changing school structure and culture does not explicitly address underlying assumptions, including what has been written about the Comer School Development Program

(Comer, 1993; Comer et al., 1996b). Consequently, many reform innovations do not succeed or achieve the desired result as the power of normative assumptions holds sway. What sets this particular group of schools apart from the numerous Comer schools that did not achieve the kinds of successes these schools have? The nine themes that characterize how these schools were able to reform through the Comer SDP represent alternative assumptions that also resonate with a growing body of research about schools that have successfully restructured.

Bureaucratic Assumptions About Structuring Schools

Schools and school districts have historically employed the bureaucratic form to organize their efforts. Structuring schools and districts according to the principles of bureaucracy assume that doing so is the most efficient way to accomplish the organization's goals. Coordination of work is achieved through power relationships formalized through a hierarchy of authority and a specified locus of control. Policies and operating procedures routinize decision making, reduce individual discretion, and discourage personal responsibility. Roles and responsibilities are narrowly defined and the supervision of work is separated from the actual work itself. This division of labor also fragments the organization and makes it difficult for participants to effectively communicate with each other (Astuto et al., 1994; Clark, 1985).

Organizing schools in this manner assumes an impersonal orientation toward the people who comprise them—students, parents, teachers, and administrators—and interferes with the development of community. Assessment of students' and teachers' work focuses on identifying and overcoming weaknesses rather than building on strengths. The parents of students from minority and lower socioeconomic statuses are viewed as deficient and a liability to their children's potential to succeed in school. Because work processes are standardized and relationships are impersonal, conflicts are viewed as aberrations that must be avoided or suppressed. Informal work norms must be controlled and/or quelled. The norm of depersonalization also convinces workers they are unable to influence the direction or context of their work (Astuto et al., 1994).

Bureaucratic organizations also assume that people need external motivation in order to perform high-quality work. This assumption can be seen in state and local accountability programs premised on rewards and punishments. Decisions about testing, curriculum, and staff development are usually made at the district level and increasingly at the state level. Doing so assumes that building-level personnel are incapable of making these decisions. The consequence of this assumption is to reduce teaching to a technical skill that merely emphasizes the delivery of prescribed instructional content, the administration of assessment, and the application of behavioral controls in the classroom. In other words, teachers are viewed solely as the means of production (Astuto et al., 1994).

The current "back to basics" movement that emphasizes high academic standards reflects an assumption that the main purpose of schooling is the acquisition of academic skills. This limited view of schooling ignores the reality that an increasing number of students are coming to school with needs in realms other than the academic. Most would agree that lack of attention to students' social, psychological, and health needs certainly inhibits their ability to perform well in academic areas. However, rather than provide comprehensive services at the school site, cooperation among the various social service agencies assumes that children's various needs will be adequately addressed. This results in a segmented rather than holistic view of students and their needs, with each agency addressing a different aspect of a child's range of concerns.

Although structuring schools this way may result in accomplishing certain educational goals, doing so sacrifices individual freedom and flexibility for control and standardization. As nonadaptable structures, bureaucracies are unable or unwilling to be responsive to the needs of individuals, who are instead expected to conform to the needs of the organization. Bureaucracy has few proponents, yet this way of organizing schools is so taken-for-granted as the best way to operate schools that it is difficult to conceive of alternatives.

Counter-Assumptions for Structuring Schools

The studies of schools that have successfully restructured reveal that they have abandoned the principles of bureaucracy. Instead, these schools have reorganized themselves according to a different set of assumptions, primarily employing those underlying the principles of democracy. How do schools apply the assumptions of democracy in practice? Darling-Hammond (1997) describes horizontal and vertical team and committee structures that ensure participation throughout the organization as characteristic of successful restructured schools. Likewise, these Comer schools adapted the multiple-team structure suggested by the SDP in order to maximize participation in their unique contexts. The interrelated nature of the teams provided a mechanism for the school's many stakeholders to effectively communicate with each other and enabled the schools to identify and pursue concerns, issues, and needs.

Dynamic leadership is needed to provide the impetus for schools to change (Elmore, Peterson, & McCarthey, 1996; Maehr & Midgley, 1996), and that was certainly the case with the powerful principals in each of these schools. Yet, organizing schools according to democratic principles assumes a broad distribution of power among participants. Equalizing power relationships opens up possibilities for communication that never before existed as individuals collaborate with each other and coordinate their work around teaching and learning. Democratic mechanisms that provide for collective decisions about the limits of individual discretion promote personal responsibility and connection to organizational-wide problems and demands.

In these schools, once the changes in structure and practice were well underway, the teams were able to balance the power of individuals who otherwise might overpower the school with their own agenda. Consistent with Comer's philosophy, interpersonal relationships in which individuals are valued and respected are critical factors within this context. Furthermore, democracies recognize that conflict is healthy and that public debate is a necessary prerequisite for reaching agreement or consensus (Astuto et al., 1994).

Schools organized around alternative assumptions also begin with a belief that people are intrinsically motivated by the work itself, as long as that work is challenging and meaningful. This counter-assumption leads to an increased sense of efficacy and the feeling that people have control over their own destinies. They are initiators of action rather than simply the means of production. This counter-assumption allowed these schools to use the SDP to make the changes in curriculum and instruction, multicultural orientation, and governance needed to respond to their students and community. While each of these schools experienced external demands for accountability, they each developed mechanisms for internal accountability premised on what is good for the students.

Instead of implementing routine work prescribed by someone else, the faculties in these restructured schools make decisions based on their professional expertise. Although the connection between the Comer process and instruction in these schools was not as strong as it could have been, many of the teachers in these Comer schools were well grounded in child and adolescent development, had access to a repertoire of methods, had a deep understanding of the content of instruction, and were able to be responsive to diverse learners. These teachers were also able to identify their own staff development needs and areas in which they would like to improve.

The counter-assumptions about people also extend to students and parents as well. Rather than viewing low-income, minority, or LEP students and parents from a deficit perspective, the faculties in these schools began with their strengths. This approach allowed these schools to address issues of racial segregation and stereotypes. Furthermore, in spite of external forces that measure a school's success solely in terms of higher test scores, these Comer schools continued to see the importance of emphasizing more than just the instructional program for their children. In fact, the Comer SDP is one of the few reform efforts that calls for comprehensive on-site services (Astuto, Clark, & Polen, 1991).

A REPRESENTATION

It is clear that the schools we studied were working with the the counter-assumptions just described. The nine themes placed within these counter-assumptions created a synergy in the schools that we believe needs to be represented in order to be fully understood. Although there is some variability among the cases, we believe it is possible and useful to try to represent the synergy in a generalized sense. We wish to be clear here. This is a representation not a model. The representation is limited by our study design and shaped by the focus on improved achievement as a key goal for these schools. Thus, although the representation puts the whole picture together it is organized by the pursuit of achievement gains. History, cultural beliefs, social practices and processes are depicted in a more linear fashion than as experienced by the research team. Nonetheless, we think it is useful to represent how things went together when using the SDP so as to emphasize the significance of the synergy in the reform of these schools. Clearly, the SDP plays a significant role in the improvement of the schools and in improved student achievement in these schools, but how this happens is rather complex.

In Figure 8.1, we represent the connections between the SDP and school success. Our argument is that these schools exist in a context of external politics, including state and district policy and leadership, accountability policy and local school-community politics. These contextual factors are a powerful force early in the school's history with the SDP, but decrease in power as the SDP becomes established. The opposite is true with school cultures, as their early effects are small compared to the influence of external politics. As the SDP becomes established, and the school community develops a sense of efficacy, the effect of school culture increases. As the school culture becomes more important, parents and community become integral to that school culture instead of being merely "external political concerns."

The SDP builds on a preexisting base of leadership and participation (e.g., faculty unity, parent involvement), and a sense of need that in part is defined by external politics. Once the SDP is established in the school, it gives the school a wider participation base and a governance mechanism. Participation and governance build a new culture in their own right, but the SDP also contributes the principles of no fault, consensus, and collaboration as well as a belief in child-centeredness. These beliefs, in turn, help generate confidence that the school can take charge of change, which results in an internal sense of accountability and, in these schools, a more multicultural perspective. By this point in the process, the school culture has been transformed. The school participants then use the culture and the governance system to address curricular and pedagogical change from a more developmental perspective. In our representation, a large arrow driving toward achievement represents this process. However, we have situated achievement outside of the arrow. This positioning is arguable, but we believe that forces partially beyond the control of the school define "student achievement." The schools work to reduce the uncertainty this brings.

The representation, of course, reflects studies of schools that have been successful with the SDP, and the synergy of context, the SDP, culture, and achievement. Without studies of schools that have had difficulty translating the

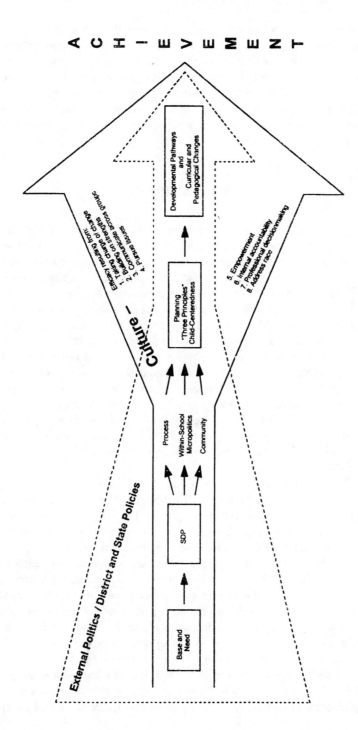

Figure 8.1. Connection between SDP and school success

SDP into positive school outcomes, we cannot specify which factors are key or where and how breakdowns in the process occur. This limits the representation to only these successful Comer schools. Nonetheless, in qualitative research, data are not usually regarded as generalizable anyway—but ideas may well be. The best use for this representation may be to generate ideas, as is true of the individual case studies and cross-site analyses in Chapter 7. There is also a final set of ideas to consider, ideas about what this study implies for the SDP and other Comer schools.

IMPLICATIONS

The complexity of this representation is important but should not obscure a key understanding about the case study schools. The SDP generates school success only when all stakeholders are committed, when people believe improvement is possible, and when schools change educational practices. Their inclusiveness of students, staff, teachers, parents, and community members in school and SDP affairs marked these schools. The schools' stakeholders reciprocated by committing to the school and the SDP. These commitments in turn translated into changes in the curricula and instructional programs. Early success with change, as Comer et al. (1996a, 1996b) predict, promotes a sense of efficacy. Child-centeredness, in whatever form it took, was key to designing instructional programs and curricula that led to gains in student performance. Although the instructional programs themselves were relatively traditional and although different teachers taught differently, the results are uniformly positive. These schools have become attractive places for people to send their children, even when they live outside the attendance areas. What these schools do *works* for the various stakeholders and for the students.

We next present implications that we believe are well-founded, given the limitations of this study's design. They should be seen as starting points for further discussion, critique, and development. The uniqueness of each of the stories of the case study schools have convinced the research team that there is not a "one best way" to do Comer. The complexity of the representation suggests that instead of following a prescribed set of instructions each Comer school should consider how it *narrates* the Comer process. By narrating, we mean describing the interconnection among factors and linking those factors to achievement outcomes, within the context of the specific school. In doing so, the school should consider the inadequacies of the representation for their story and ask what needs to be altered in the representation to reflect their story. During this reflective process, the school should consider what needs to be added to or altered in their story to make the narrative complete and compelling. The SDP at Yale University and Comer schools should ask: How can we use the implications of this study to create more and better stories of successful urban schools? We offer the following implications in the same spirit. In each section, we first summarize our findings and then explain the implications.

Leading Comer Schools

In each of these stories, a dynamic, relatively new principal was central to implementing the SDP and in influencing the school staff to take charge of change. This confirms conventional wisdom about what kind of principal is necessary for reform to take hold. However, once fully implemented, the SDP redistributes leadership more equally among many players. The SDP determines the issues on which the principal will lead—a balancing process that is analogous to legislative and executive branches of government. The principal also has a set of other responsibilities that we enumerate in Chapter 7. These responsibilities include promoting the school's culture and climate, as well as insuring faithful adherence to the SDP. In the case study schools, the result is a balancing of a strong principal who could otherwise become overbearing. The principal continues to lead but the decisions he or she enacts are the result of the SPMT's participatory process. The ancillary responsibilities he or she assumes help to bolster the power of the SDP. The case studies also reveal that after implementation of the SDP a different leader can be effective, as at West High. Nonetheless, the story of Merrit School dramatically demonstrates that the principal is responsible for the SDP realizing its promise. When a clique captures the SDP so that it becomes exclusionary, it may be necessary for the principal to regenerate the base of faculty unity. How this is done is very important. At Merrit, the ruling clique's dissatisfaction with the changes in the school made their changing jobs a reasonable option. The principal arranged for the district to offer them attractive jobs, and then reconstituted a faculty committed to the SDP. This move both avoided a power struggle and helped to maintain a lower profile principal's role.

The SDP requires sophisticated leadership. Yet few administrator preparation programs develop the nuanced understanding of power and participation the SDP requires of principals. The SDP's principal training needs to counter both conventional wisdom and prior administrator education as it promotes understanding of how their role will need to change. After training, principals should receive follow-up consultation on site. A system of peer observation and advice would enable the principals to help each other develop the needed sophistication.

The SDP in the case study schools enabled school staff to develop a broader and more participative definition of leadership. The SPMTs should work with the principals to determine what leadership is needed, when, and by whom. The Comer principles of no fault, consensus, and collaboration will greatly facilitate this process. Furthermore, the principal will play a decidedly difficult role in insuring the faithful use of the principles to discuss her or his own leadership. An outside facilitator may be required.

Creating Faculty Unity

As noted in the stories and the representation, a base and a perception of need are both essential to the implementation of the Comer Process. Faculty must become unified either before SDP implementation or early in the implementation. External threats can provide powerful means to achieve unity as we saw as with the shared ordeal that unified the staff at Gregory School. Successful resolution of the threats develops the sense of efficacy that is so important in these schools' stories. Yet in the case study schools, the use of external threats coincides with a reconstitution of the faculty. New faculty who were committed to the principal, school, and the SDP replaced teachers who would not commit to the SDP. The SDP maintains the unity as staff actually make changes and see that those changes have desirable effects. When the SDP takes charge of change, teacher unity links to efficacy and a sense of internal accountability. As noted earlier, faculty unity can dissipate, and if this happens it is necessary to reconstitute a unified faculty committed to the SDP.

The implication is that the SDP can bolster faculty unity but that it is a primary responsibility of the principal to generate and guard it. Because it is common for schools to have cliques and factions (see, e.g., Ball, 1987), it may be that having or not having cliques is a key distinction between schools that use the SDP to generate success and those who do not. Generating diagnostic tools that reveal the micropolitics of the school may help principals and staffs know whether or not they are ready for Comer. These tools can also be used during SDP implementation and training to check the state of faculty unity. Faculty unity is an intermediate goal that needs to translate into taking charge of change. Unity, like the SDP itself, is one component of creating successful urban schools.

The research team did not see systematic processes in these schools that would allow teachers to reflect on their classroom practices. Faculty unity, coupled with a sense of efficacy, should make it possible for teachers to open their classrooms to each other. Peer observation systems often are more evaluative than reflective in that the observer is asked to comment on the teaching of the observed teacher. A more reflective process would invert this procedure. Rather than requiring the observer to comment on the observed, a reflective process of peer observation would ask the observer to learn from the observation to improve his or her own teaching. Peer observation, of course, can be divisive for faculty. The decision to try such a process must be the result of the overall comprehensive planning effort and the normal Comer decision-making mechanisms and principles. It should also reflect child-centeredness and the developmental pathways. Using faculty unity as a tool to change classroom practice is the next step in the case study schools.

Rallying the Whole Village

"Rallying the whole village," of course, is one of James Comer's ways of explaining the SDP, and it has a special meaning in the case study schools. School staff repeatedly told us that they were "bringing the community into the process," but in practice they meant much more than merely bringing parents and the community into the school. Even Epstein's (1995) six categories of parent involvement (parenting, communicating, volunteering, learning at home, decision making, collaborating with community) fail to capture how these schools used the Comer Process to involve the parents and community. The schools brokered a wide range of services for parents and community members, and in doing so became not only part of a more collaborative services system but a social institution advocating for the community in the local political sphere. In themselves, these are remarkable ways to conceive of community and parent involvement, but the schools also took Comer's idea of rallying the village literally. The schools use the SDP to organize parents and the community into a viable force that can influence the school's relations with the school district and local government. The schools mobilized this force repeatedly and effectively. Not only are parents involved, they are *literally* empowered.

The implication of this is that making parents welcome and collaborating with other community agencies are only the first steps in a series of steps. The SDP should help school staff examine the fuller process which at a minimum includes: (a) bringing the community in; (b) using the community as a resource in the school and classrooms; (c) brokering services to the parents and community; (d) advocating for the community; and (e) mobilizing the community in the service of the school and students. Anyon (1997) argues that the schools need to go beyond their own mission to mobilize the parents and community in the service of interests outside of the school, "to restructure the city environment itself" (p. 13). As daunting as this challenge may appear, it is the next logical step.

It should be remembered that being successful in these mobilizations is essential to maintaining a sense of empowerment. In the case study schools, the principal plays a key role in both choosing the political battles and in designing the political struggle, often in consultation with other community leaders. Principal and parent training that is part of the SDP should facilitate principals' and parents' sharing what they have learned about effective political mobilization. This is a rare art that needs to be nourished for the SDP to be effective in creating successful urban schools.

Bringing the Children In

The Comer Process focuses schools on students, but the students become more beneficiaries than participants. The notable exception to this is the way Merritt

School uses the SDP as a model for student government. This is a practice that other schools should consider for fostering student involvement, developing student leadership skills, and bringing students into the community as participants as well as beneficiaries.

There is even less evidence that the SDP is being used in classrooms even though SDP training promotes such use. Although teachers think about child-centeredness and the developmental pathways, it is not evident that they consider the Comer Process as a model for classroom governance. What is clear, however, is that the students identify with their schools and their successes and see themselves as "getting smarter." These are important accomplishments in formerly dispirited schools that used a deficit model to guide their approach to children. Nonetheless, the research team sees Comer as a powerful model for classroom governance that is unrealized.

Adapting the Comer Process to the classroom, of course, should be guided by a developmental understanding of what is appropriate for students. SDP trainers may need to organize a special training program about implementing Comer in the classroom. At a minimum, this training should be about classroom governance, but next we argue that it should also involve reconceptualizing pedagogy.

Creating a Pedagogical Focus

The case study schools have found the Comer Process to be helpful in realigning curricula and redesigning instructional programs. This has been a key to translating the SDP into gains in student performance. Accountability policy presses for a narrowing of pedagogical focus to what is tested, and the schools have adjusted their curricula and instructional programs to be successful on these terms. The schools have also somewhat corrected for this by elaborating the curricula to better address the developmental pathways. Although different schools have different contexts and student bodies, each has developed new programs and improved existing ones. Similarly, each of the schools use the SDP to address race and language diversity, while working to reduce race and ethnic separations in the school and the community. Balancing inclusion and effective instructional programs is part of the ongoing curricula and instructional deliberations. Nonetheless, rather traditional instruction is the norm in these schools. As noted earlier, this has worked and has the support of a wide range of stakeholders, but the schools indicate they will continue to work on pedagogy.

Creating a pedagogical focus has two implications for the SDP. First, it may be appropriate to consider adding a fourth mechanism, an Instructional Team, as was done at West High. Creating this mechanism would institutionalize a pedagogical focus within the Comer Process. To avoid teams becoming teacher-controlled, it would be necessary to have a broad representation of parents, community, and students. Second, a pedagogical focus must go beyond decisions about curricula and instructional programs and venture into the class-rooms. As noted in the cross-site analyses, teachers in inner-city schools are often less well-trained, have fewer materials, and have had to adapt to teaching in disruptive and demoralizing situations with minimal district support. The tra-ditional instruction that we observed may be the result of these conditions.

To its credit, the SDP has enabled educators to teach to the limits of their capabilities. What is needed is to expand the capacity of these teachers. The Comer Process should allow teachers to take risks and to learn what will further improve their instruction. A peer observation process, as described pre-viously, would be a place to start. Yet a peer observation process does not bring new ideas about instruction to the school. Teachers need to learn and experi-ment with new pedagogical ideas to expand their capacities. Although the case study schools all sought out professional development opportunities for their teachers, more is needed. At Trivette, the faculty is exploring district-sponsored instructional reforms that would be implemented in all classrooms. For some schools, broadly instituted instructional reforms may provide a solution, but for others forcing uniformity of classroom instruction may create factions among the faculty that serve to undercut the SDP. In such schools, it may be appropri-ate to have individual teachers sample a range of alternatives and choose one for their individual improvement. This, of course, does not generate a unified class-room pedagogy, but avoiding a factionalized teaching staff is a high priority. Another source of ideas may come by expanding the existing relationships with colleges and universities beyond student placements and student teaching. Comer schools offer attractive partnerships for higher education, and these should be exploited. The Comer Process does present some limits on the types of instruction that are appropriate because of its developmental focus. Any efforts to improve either the instructional programs or classroom instruction must include expanding the use of the developmental pathways in creating a pedagogical focus.

Articulating the Teams

The SDP depends on the Parent Team, the SSST, and the SPMT working close-ly together. Input from the Parent Team and the SSST flows into the SPMT and the development of the comprehensive school plan. The Parent Team largely provides input into the process and becomes mobilized to support the school. We have less evidence the SPMT actively works to benefit the parents them-selves. The SSST is charged with coordinating services to serve the needs of individual students and demonstrating that the school cares about the child. On occasion, the SSST addresses schoolwide needs, as with the Health Fair at Gregory School. The SPMT may direct the SSST to these efforts, but it seems that the SSST rarely uses its experiences and data to identify patterns that may help inform pedagogical discussions in the SPMT.

The teams need better two-way articulation. The lesson from the political empowerment of parents and the community is that the teams must be used for more than input. The Parent Team and the SPMT should review the Parent Team's mission regularly to assure that it is being used to its capacity. The SPMT also needs to consider what it can do to assist parents beyond working effectively with their children. The same is true for the SSST, but the implication is that the SSST needs to place more effort on identifying issues that impact the instructional programs and curricula. Both teams will need training to support these expanded efforts.

Developing a Comer Culture

The SDP has restructured and helped build a new culture for the case study schools. The Comer Process, of course, comes with a set of beliefs that alter the school's culture. The developmental perspective; the principles of no fault, consensus, and collaboration; the focus on participation and inclusion; and the use of data-based planning to organize school efforts all are part of the cultures of the case study schools. In turn, the SDP and the cultural beliefs central to it play a part in generating another set of beliefs. These beliefs are, at a minimum, taking charge of change, a sense of efficacy, internal accountability, and multiculturalism. The representation discussed earlier in this chapter shows culture to have a large effect on the achievement gains realized in these schools. These cultural beliefs are powerful because they are, in fact, beliefs about power. The Comer culture in the case study schools is generative. People do remarkable things because they believe they can—and because they believe it is their responsibility to do remarkable things.

Developing a Comer culture is neither easy nor assured. If faculty unity is lost, so is the power of the culture. If a political struggle is lost, demonstrating that the school cannot take charge of change, then the set of beliefs about power comes unraveled, and so on. Furthermore, culture is hard to control and manipulate. Indeed, efforts to promote beliefs in the absence of an undergirding lived experience is largely futile and may generate cynicism and/or resistance. The implication is that although culture can be discussed in training, it cannot be changed by training alone. It is up to the school principal and the SDP in the school to make a new lived reality for school participants. The cultural beliefs then can be developed by inviting participants to reflect on and interpret the experiences. After schools have had some successes, training or facilitation can play an important role in naming the new beliefs and deepening their meaning. As the SDP training emphasizes, it is what people do with the Comer Process that makes improvement possible, and this is certainly the case with developing a Comer culture.

Mobilizing School District Support

The districts provide case study schools with extra funds, training, facilitation, and political protection. The districts are proud of the successes of these schools. Yet, district support is in many ways limited to the tenure of the superintendent. Changes in superintendents bring new emphases and threaten the continuity of school-level reforms.

The implication is that district support is vital to implementing any new reform, including the SDP. Moreover, sustaining the reform is conditional on ongoing district support in at least three ways. First, although it is often thought that the costs of reform can be scaled back over time, that has not been the case with these schools. They need the continued funding from the district and more. These schools spend considerable effort getting grants to underwrite the costs of reform. School districts tend to view the funding of reforms as discretionary and temporary. For Comer to produce positive outcomes, and to sustain these improvements, districts need to consider the increases to the school budgets as permanent. Second, the principals in these schools do not "play by the rules" of the bureaucracy. When they need something to happen, the principals rally the village, call in debts, and construct and use alliances. This, of course, can lead to recalcitrance and retaliation by central office administrators. Superintendents should focus on the bottom line: Is the school making progress? If so, then the superintendent should look out for the school's interests in the central bureaucracy. Finally, principal turnover should be considered a major threat to the SDP in any school. When a principal leaves a Comer school, a superintendent needs to choose a new principal who is an advocate of Comer and has the sophisticated leadership skills the SDP demands.

Sustaining Success

The research team has been consistently impressed with the fact that these schools have, in many ways, escaped their defining context. The research on education makes the implicit and often explicit association of "urban" with "problem" (Miron, 1996). Urban schools are understood to be resource limited, physically decayed, psychologically demoralizing, and serving the least adept students and communities. Yet, the five schools we have studied defy these characterizations. This is not to say that these schools do not have challenges to face or have sufficient funds to fully educate their pupils. Rather, it is that these schools are no longer like other schools nearby. They are urban, but they are not a problem for the staff, parents, or community. As one person noted, "Comer makes us resilient to deal with the stresses. . . ." We have been around urban schools long enough to know that Comer schools are not the only schools that dissociate "urban" from "problem." It is nonetheless impressive to us that these schools have not only escaped the defining context of their location, they have escaped their own histories as "schools in trouble." Yet, we do not want to underestimate the power of the urban context nor the ubiquity of change for these schools. These are what make the accomplishments of these schools all too fragile.

Changes in district priorities and support, principal turnover, failures in political struggles, and any number of other factors all can destroy the culture and the successes of these schools. Yet, when you talk with teachers, parents, and others it is clear that the schools studied here are empowered, and the SDP has played a major role in this empowerment. With Comer, they believe they can deal effectively with whatever challenges are presented to them. In urban schools, this is a significant accomplishment.

The principals of these schools see both the fragility of success and the power of the people in the schools. They hope that the school has such a strong investment in the SDP that it would survive if they left the school. West High offers hope that this is possible, but also underscores that the successor principal needs to be committed to the SDP and to able respect where the school is in the Comer Process, facilitating its growth from that point. Merrit School testifies to the fragility of faculty unity, and the role of the principal in regenerating that unity and the SDP. The research team has been asked repeatedly: Is it the SDP or the principal that makes the difference? Our answer is *both*. Alone, neither is sufficient. Sustaining the successes of these schools is dependent both on a principal knowing how to use power and on the SDP governing the school and focusing on improved curricula and instruction. Aligned, the principal and the SDP accomplish the restructuring and reculturing necessary to successfully reform schools. However, a school, once reformed, is not reformed forever. Schools need a participatory process and leadership that sustains reform, and the energy and the power that successful reform generates. The SDP gave these schools the process, and schools then generated the power.

THE PROMISE OF THE SDP: CONCLUSION

We think the best way to conclude this book is to consider the promise of the SDP as a vehicle of school reform. We have been careful to argue that these schools should not be taken as representative of all Comer schools. They were selected precisely because they are especially successful. We have also argued that Comer's SDP precedes the current reform era and springs from a different source—concerns about urban education, people of color, and equity. Indeed, these schools work from different assumptions. Nonetheless, people interested in the SDP will undoubtably ask: How does Comer in general compare to what is known about promising school reforms? This moves us beyond these five schools.

Shields and Knapp (1997) report on a national study of school-based reform, and conclude that promising school-based reforms have six dimensions: scope, focus on curriculum and instruction, time frame, focus of authority, collaborative engagement of participants, and professional development opportunities. We believe that the School Development Program can be classified as a promising reform using their criteria.

Scope. Shields and Knapp (1997) argue that "some school-based reforms are more ambitious than others" (p. 289). Their research demonstrates a promising reform is one that is neither too narrow nor too comprehensive. Each end is an extreme. Narrow reforms accomplish only one of two things; comprehensive reforms are impractical and daunting to participants.

Our research shows that the SDP is within the promising range. Although the SDP offers a governance system, child centeredness and a set of principles for decision making, it does not require a wholesale revamping of the school and its curricula. Like other promising reforms, the SDP is of moderate scope.

Focus on curriculum and instruction. Shields and Knapp indicate that reforms vary considerably in their attention to classroom instruction and curricula. Some reforms focus on governance or discipline, whereas others make curricula and instruction a sole focus. The SDP is unusual in that it promotes child development as a central focus and allows educators to decide how best to address the development of their students. Promising reforms, according to Shields and Knapp, are relatively focused on curricula and instruction. Although the schools studied here tended to develop this focus, it may be that the difference between these successful schools and other Comer schools is the focus on curricula and instruction. On this dimension, the SDP may not be as promising as some other reforms.

Time frame. Although school-based reform takes time, Shields and Knapp argue that reforms and schools that wish to reform have varying time frames. Some want to change many things at once; others wish to be more deliberative and planful. Nonetheless, their research shows that a longer time frame is more promising than a short time frame.

The SDP itself offers no timetable for reform. Indeed, the schedule of its professional development indicates that reform takes time to be effective. The schools we studied implemented the SDP rather quickly but acknowledge the fragility of their accomplishments. This, in turn, means that for the SDP, reform is never fully accomplished but rather is always ongoing, much like other promising reforms.

Focus of authority. Many of the recent reform initiatives have been top-down. Schools have been forced to reform by state or district initiatives. Yet

Shields and Knapp report that many schools have been able to "accept and assume" (p. 290) such initiatives and make them their own. Thus in their view, promising reforms are both top-down *and* bottom-up.

The SDP typically has a district-level initiative to provide professional development, liaison, and support. Yet, the real action of the SDP takes place at the school and community level. It, like other promising reforms, is both top-down and bottom-up. Again, the SDP seems to be quite promising as a reform.

Collaborative engagement. All reforms have a rhetoric of collaboration and communication, but whether collaboration occurs in the *work* of the schools is another matter entirely. Shields and Knapp found that promising reforms move beyond a rhetoric of collaboration to collaborative practice.

Collaborative practice is one of the mainstays of the SDP. The mechanism (the three teams) and principles (consensus, collaboration, no fault) are explicitly about putting collaborative practice in place. In the schools we studied, people were so collaboratively engaged that there were no political factions within the schools. Although this may well be an exceptional accomplishment, the fact remains that Comer schools are highly collaborative.

Professional development opportunities. School-based reforms vary in the professional development they offer. Some offer rich and sustained opportunities; others offer either initial or sporadic opportunities. Promising reforms lean toward the former over the latter.

The SDP offers initial and advanced training at Yale. This is also coupled with a Yale-based district facilitator, a local-district SDP facilitator, and local training. It is especially noteworthy that the SDP puts an emphasis on developing parents that many reforms do not. In short, the SDP seems promising on this dimension as well.

Our conclusion is that although the schools we studied are exceptionally successful, the SDP has all but one of the dimensions of promising school-based reforms. The exception is the focus on curricula and instruction. This seems to issue a challenge to the SDP. The challenge is how best to help schools better translate the SDP's focus on child development into a focus on classroom instruction. The Comer schools studied here accomplished this, and much more. It is time to disseminate these accomplishments widely. As Comer acknowledges, this will ultimately have to be the work of schools themselves if they are to help the kids to get smarter.

References

Adkins, A., Awsumb, C., Noblit, G., & Richards, P. (Eds.). (1998). *Working together? Grounded perspectives on interagency collaboration*. Cresskill: NJ: Hampton Press.

Anderson, E. (1988). *The education of blacks in the south, 1860-1985*. Chapel Hill: University of North Carolina Press.

Anyon, J. (1997). *Ghetto schooling: A political economy of urban educational reform*. New York: Teachers College Press.

Astuto, T.A., Clark, D.L., & Polen, D.A. (1991). *Alternative designs for restructured schools*. Paper presented at the Annual Meeting of the American Educational Research Association, Chicago, IL.

Astuto, T.A., Clark, D.L., Read, A.M., McGree, K., & Fernandez, L.d.P. (1994). *Roots of reform: Challenging the assumptions that control change in education*. Indianapolis, IN: Phi Delta Kappa Educational Foundation.

Ball, S. (1987). *The micropolitics of the school*. London: Methuen.

Beck, L.G., & Murphy, J. (1996). *The four imperatives of a successful school*. Thousand Oaks, CA: Corwin Press.

Berliner, D.C., & Biddle, B.J. (1997). *The manufactured crisis: Myths, fraud, and the attack on America's public schools*. White Plains, NY: Longman.

Bracey, G. W. (1997). *Setting the record straight: Responses to misconceptions about public education in the United States.* Alexandria, VA: Association for Supervision and Curriculum Development.

Clark, D.L. (1985). Emerging paradigms in organization theory and research. In Y.S. Lincoln (Ed.), *Organizational theory and inquiry: The paradigm revolution* (pp. 43-78). Beverly Hills, CA: Sage.

Collins, R. (1982). *Sociological insight.* New York: Oxford University Press.

Comer, J.P. (1988). Educating poor minority children. *Scientific American, 259*(5), 42-48.

Comer, J.P. (1993). *School power: Implications of a school intervention project* (2nd ed.). New York: The Free Press.

Comer, J.P., & Haynes, N.M. (1992). *Summary of School Development Program effects.* Unpublished manuscript.

Comer, J.P., Haynes, N.M., & Joyner, E. (1996a). The School Development Program. In J. Comer, N.M. Haynes, E.T. Joyner, & M. Ben-Avie (Eds.), *Rallying the whole village: The Comer Process for reforming education* (pp. 1-26). New York: Teachers College Press.

Comer, J.P., Haynes, N.M., Joyner, E.T., & Ben-Avie, M. (Eds.). (1996b). *Rallying the whole village: The Comer Process for reforming education.* New York: Teachers College Press.

Corbett, H.D., & Wilson, B.L. (1991). *Testing, reform, and rebellion.* Norwood, NJ: Ablex Publishing.

Cuban, L. (1988). Why do some reforms persist? *Educational Administration Quarterly, 24*(3), 329-335.

Darling-Hammond, L. (1997). *The right to learn: A blueprint for creating schools that work.* San Francisco: Jossey-Bass.

Darling-Hammond, L., & Wise, A.E. (1985). Beyond standardization: State standards and school improvement. *Elementary School Journal, 85*, 313-336.

Delpit, L. (1995). *Other people's children: Cultural conflict in the classroom.* New York: The New Press.

Dempsey, V.O., & Noblit, G.W. (1995). Cultural ignorance and school desegregation: A community narrative. In M. Shujaa (Ed.), *Beyond desegregation: The politics of African-American schooling* (pp. 115-137). Thousand Oaks, CA: Corwin Press.

DuBois, W.E.B. (1935). *The souls of black folk.* Scarborough, NY: Signet Books.

Elmore, R.F., Peterson, P.L., & McCarthey, S.J. (1996). *Restructuring in the classroom: Teaching, learning, and school organization.* San Francisco: Jossey-Bass.

Emmons, C., Owen, S.V., Haynes, N.M., & Comer, J.P. (1992, March). *A causal model of the effects of school climate, classroom climate, academic self-concept, suspension, and absenteeism on academic achievement.* Paper presented at the Annual Meeting of the Eastern Educational Research Association, Hilton Head, SC.

Epstein, J. (1995). School-family-community partnerships. *Phi Delta Kappan, 76*(9), 701-711.

Fiske, E.B. (1991). *Smart schools, smart kids: Why do some schools work?* New York: Simon & Schuster.

Giddens, A. (1979). *Central problems of social theory.* Berkeley: University of California Press.

Glaser, B. G., & Strauss A. (1967). *The discovery of grounded theory. Strategies for qualitative research.* Chicago: Aldine.

Goens, G.A., & Clover, S.I.R. (1991). *Mastering school reform.* Needham Heights, MA: Allyn & Bacon.

Haynes, N.M., & Bility, K. (1994). Evaluating school development. In *School Development Program research monograph.* New Haven, CT: Yale Child Study Center.

Hawley, A. (1988). Missing pieces of the educational reform agenda: Or why the first and second waves may miss the boat. *Educational Administration Quarterly, 24*(4), 416-437.

House, E.R. (1977). *The logic of evaluative argument.* Los Angeles: University of California, Center for the Study of Evaluation.

Kent, J.D. (1987). A not too distant past. *The Educational Forum, 51*(2), 123-135.

Kimball, B. (1986). *Orators and philosophers: A history of the idea of liberal education.* New York: Teachers College Press.

Kozol, J. (1991). *Savage inequalities.* New York: Corwin Publishers.

Maehr, M.L., & Midgley, C. (1996). *Transforming school cultures.* Boulder, CO: Westview Press.

Merriam, S.B. (1988). *Case study research in education: A qualitative approach.* San Francisco: Jossey-Bass Publishers.

Miles, M.B., & Huberman, A.M. (1984). *Qualitative data analysis: A sourcebook of new methods.* Beverly Hills, CA: Sage.

Miron, L.F. (1996). *The social construction of urban schooling: Situating the crisis.* Cresskill, NJ: Hampton Press.

Muncey, D.E., & McQuillan, P.J. (1996). *Reform and resistance in classrooms: An ethnographic view of the Coalition of Essential Schools.* New Haven, CT: Yale University Press.

Murphy, J. (1990). The educational reform movement of the 1980s: A comprehensive analysis. In J. Murphy (Ed.), *The educational reform movement of the 1980s: Perspectives and cases.* Berkeley, CA: McCutcheon Publishing.

National Commission on Excellence in Education. (1983). *A nation at risk: The imperative for educational reform.* Washington, DC: Government Printing Office.

Neufeld, B., & LaBue, M.A. (1994). *The implementation of the School Development Program in Hartford.* Cambridge, MA: Education Matters.

152   References

Noblit, G.W., & Dempsey, V.O. (1996). *The social construction of virtue: The moral life of schools.* New York: State University of New York Press.
Noblit, G.W., & Hare, R.D. (1988). *Meta-ethnography: Synthesizing qualitative studies.* Beverly Hills, CA: Sage.
Noblit, G.W., & Johnston, B. (Eds.). (1982). *The school principal and school desegregation.* Springfield, IL: Charles Thomas Press.
Ogbu, J.U. (1978). *Minority education and caste: The American system in cross-cultural perspective.* New York: Academic Press.
Ogbu, J.U. (1995). Cultural remedies for school segregation: A social science statement to the US Supreme Court in Missouri v. Jenkins. *The Urban Review, 27,* 189-206.
Patton, M.Q. (1990). *Qualitative evaluation and research.* Newbury Park, CA: Sage.
Sarason, S.B. (1997). *Barometers of change: Individual, educational, and social transformation.* Jossey-Bass: San Francisco.
Sergiovanni, T.J. (1987). *The principalship: A reflective practice perspective.* Boston: Allyn & Bacon.
Shields, P.M., & Knapp, M.S. (December, 1997). The promise and limits of school-based reform: A national snapshot. *Phi Delta Kappan,* 288-294.
Shujaa, M.J. (Ed.). (1994). *Too much schooling, too little education: A paradox of black life in white societies.* Trenton, NJ: Africa World Press.
Siddle Walker, E.V. (1993). Caswell County Training School, 1933-1969. *Harvard Educational Review, 63,* 161-181.
Smith, J.P. (1996). Efficacy and teaching mathematics by telling: A challenge for reform. *Journal for Research in Mathematics Education, 27*(4), 387-402.
Steele, C.M. (1992, April). Race and the schooling of Black Americans. *Atlantic Monthly,* 68-78.
Steele, C.M. (1993, March 20). *African Americans and disidentification.* Paper presented at the Lilly Teaching Fellows Colloquium on Teaching, Chapel Hill, NC.
Steele, C.M. (1995). Stereotype threat and the intellectual test performance of African Americans. *Journal of Personality and Social Psychology, 69*(5), 797-811.
Steele, C.M. (1997). A threat in the air: How stereotypes shape intellectual identity and performance. *American Psychologist, 52*(6), 613-629.
Tyack, D., Lowe, R., & Hansot, E. (1984). *Public schools in hard times: The great depression and recent years.* Cambridge, MA: Harvard University Press.
Valdes, G. (1986). *Con respecto* [with respect]. New York: Teachers College Press.
Villenas, S. (1996). The colonizer/colonized Chicana ethnographer: Identity, marginalization, and co-optation in the field. *Harvard Educational Review, 66*(4), 711-731.

Warren, D. (1990). Passage of rites: On the history of educational reform in the United States. In J. Murphy (Ed.), *The educational reform movement of the 1980s: Perspectives and cases* (pp. 57-81). Berkeley, CA: McCutcheon.

Washington, B.T. (1965). Up from slavery. Reprinted in J. Franklin (Ed.), *Three Negro classics* (pp. 23-206). New York: Avon.

Weick, K.E. (1976). Educational organizations as loosely coupled systems. *Administrative Science Quarterly, 21,* 1-19.

Zeichner, K.M. (1991). Contradictions and tensions in the professionalization of teaching and the democratization of schools. *Teachers College Record, 92,* 363-379.

Author Index

Subject Index